LIBERTY
TO THE
CAPTIVES

Praise be to the Lord,
who has not let us be torn by their teeth.

We have escaped like a bird out of the fowler's snare;
the snare has been broken, and we have escaped.

Our help is in the name of the Lord,
the maker of heaven and earth.

Psalm 124

About the Author

Mark Durie is a theologian, human rights activist and pastor of an Anglican church. He has published many articles and books on Christian-Muslim relations, religious freedom and the language and culture of the Acehnese. He is a graduate of the Australian National University (BA Hons, PhD) and the Australian College of Theology (DipTh, BTh Hons, ThD). After holding visiting appointments at the University of Leiden, Massachusetts Institute of Technology, Stanford University, and the University of California at Los Angeles and Santa Cruz, he became Head of the Department of Linguistics and Language Studies at the University of Melbourne, was elected a Fellow of the Australian Academy of the Humanities in 1992, and awarded an Australian Bicentennial Medal in 2001 for contributions to research.

By the same author

The Third Choice: Islam, Dhimmitude and Freedom
Deror Books 2010

Which God? Jesus, Holy Spirit, God
in Christianity and Islam
Deror Books 2013

For more information on Mark Durie's books:

www.markdurie.com

LIBERTY
TO THE
CAPTIVES

Freedom from Islam and Dhimmitude
through the Cross

Revised Edition

MARK DURIE

db

DEROR BOOKS

Printed in Australia, USA and Great Britain.
ISBN: 978-0-9874691-0-6

Deror Books
www.derorbooks.com

CONTENTS

Acknowledgements

I am grateful for the support of so many individuals, whose feedback, advice and encouragement have contributed so much to the genesis of this small book. Without their help, it could never have been written.

I particularly wish to thank the Mosques and Miracles team for all their support over the years and providing a context to trial the prayers renouncing the *dhimma*.

I welcome any suggestions for improving this resource for Christian ministry, especially regarding the ministry prayers found in the final chapters.

Mark Durie, March 2013.

On referencing

This volume has been deliberately set out using a minimum of references and footnotes. For full details and references on the subject matter of chapters 2-4, please consult *The Third Choice: Islam, dhimmitude and freedom*.

References to the Quran use the abbreviation Q — e.g. Q9:29 refers to *Sura* 9:29, which is chapter 9, verse 29 of the Quran.

Quranic citations are from the translation of Arthur J. Arberry, but the verse numbering follows the translation of Yusuf Ali.

Permission to use the prayers

The prayers in chapters 7 and 8 may be reprinted provided that the publisher is informed (via www.derorbooks. com), and the following attribution is included:

CHAPTER I

The Need to Renounce Islam

One of the pressing needs of many people in the world today is to renounce Islam. *Liberty to the Captives* has been written to meet this need. It provides tools—information and prayers—to help Christians become free from the controlling spiritual influence of Islam.

The key idea of this book is that Islam's spiritual power is exercised through two covenants, known as the *shahada* and the *dhimma*. The *shahada* binds Muslims and the *dhimma* binds non-Muslims to conditions determined by Islamic law.

This book explains:

- How a person, who was a Muslim but has chosen to follow Christ, can renounce and be set free from covenantal allegiance to the *shahada* and all that it entails.

- How someone can claim freedom as a Christian and be released from the demeaning inferiority imposed on non-Muslims by Islamic sharia law through the *dhimma*.

Christians can claim their rightful freedom from both these covenants by renouncing them. For this very purpose, prayers for renouncing Islam—liturgies of freedom—are provided here.

The Two Covenants

The Arabic word *Islam* means 'submission' or 'surrender'. The faith of Muhammad makes two kinds of submission available to the world. One is the surrender of the convert, who accepts the religion of Islam. The other is the surrender of the non-Muslim, who submits to Islamic subjugation without conversion.

- The covenant of the convert is the *shahada*, the Muslim creed. This is a confession of faith in the unity of Allah, the prophethood of Muhammad, and all that these entail.

- The covenant of the non-Muslim who surrenders to Islamic political dominance is the *dhimma*. This is an institution of Islamic law which determines the status of Christians and others who choose not to convert to Islam but are compelled to live under its rule.

Islam's demand that humankind submit, either by confessing the *shahada,* or accepting the *dhimma*, must be resisted.

Many Christians would not find it surprising that someone who has left the Muslim faith to follow Christ might need to renounce Islam. Fewer may grasp that Christians who have never been Muslims can nevertheless come under the spiritual influence of Islamic dominance, and may need to specifically take their personal stand against the claims of the *dhimma* pact, rejecting the fear and inferiority status that Islam seeks to impose upon them as non-Muslims.

Liberty to the Captives offers a concise explanation of the principles behind these twin covenants of dominance— the *shahada* and the *dhimma*—and invites the reader to consider Christ, the power of his life, and the spiritual resources for freedom which he has secured through the cross. Finally Biblical principles are given and prayers provided which enable the reader to claim for themselves the freedom which Christ has already secured on their behalf.

Transfer of Sovereignty

Many Islamic theologians make much of the idea of sovereignty: they emphasize that sovereignty is 'only for Allah'. By this they mean that *sharia* law should have preeminence over all other principles of justice or power.

A key idea of this book is that followers of Christ have the right and indeed a duty to renounce other forms of spiritual sovereignty.

In a Christian understanding, turning to Christ means rejecting and renouncing all spiritual claims over one's soul, except those of Christ. Paul in his letter to the Colossians, described coming to faith in Christ as a transfer from one kingdom to another:

> For he has rescued us from the dominion of darkness and brought us into the kingdom of the Son he loves, in whom we have redemption, the forgiveness of sins. (Colossians 1:13-14)

The spiritual strategy proposed in this book is an application of this principle of transferal from one kingdom to another. The Christian believer, as an integral part of their redemption, has come under Christ's rule. As such he or she is no longer subject to the principles of the 'dominion of darkness'. For believers to claim and own this freedom for themselves—which is their birthright—in opposition to Islam's claims, they need to understand what they have been transferred out **from**, and what they have been transferred in**to**. This book offers this knowledge to the reader and provides believers with resources which enable them to apply it.

The Sword is not the Answer

There are many ways to resist Islam's will to dominate. This can involve a wide range of actions, including political and community action, human rights advocacy, academic inquiry, and the use of media to communicate the truth. For some communities and nations there are times when a military response may be necessary.

When Muhammad commissioned his followers to take his faith to the world, he instructed them to offer **three** choices to non-Muslims. One was conversion— the *shahada*—another was political surrender—the *dhimma*—but another choice was 'the sword'—to fight for their lives, killing and being killed, as the Arabic word *qātilū*, used in the Quran to describe this struggle, implies (see e.g. Q9:29, 2:190, 2:193, 2:217, 9:111).

Yet the path of resistance to *jihad* brings spiritual perils, quite apart from the possibility of defeat at the hands of Muslims. When the Christians of the Old World embarked on defensive resistance to Islamic conquest, a struggle which was to last more than a millennium—it was almost eight centuries until the Reconquista of the Iberian peninsula was completed—they were transformed by the experience, and not always for the better. It was barely seven years after the Saracens sacked Rome in 846—and more than a century after the Arab invasion and occupation of Andalusia—that Pope Leo in 853 AD promised the assurance of paradise to those who gave their lives defending Christian churches and cities against the Arabs. More than three centuries later Pope Gregory VII extended forgiveness of sins to anyone who died fighting for the aggressive extension of Christian power into the lands of non-believers. Thus was the Holy War dogma of the crusades established, a 'Christian jihad' theology mimicking Islam, which was exported by the Conquistadors to the New World, with bloody results.

Today Christians no longer preach 'Holy War', but the fact that so much of the Christian world got caught up in the 'Christian jihad' heresy developed as a direct response to the theological agenda of Islam, should be a salutary lesson of the risks involved in resisting Islam.

The root of the power of Islam is not military or political, but spiritual. Islam makes what are in essence **spiritual** demands, institutionalized in sharia law through the institutions of the *shahada* and the *dhimma*. For this reason, the resources offered here to resist and liberate people from Islam are spiritual. They are designed to be put to use by Christian believers, applying a Biblical understanding of the cross to come into freedom.

'Not by human power'

In the book of Daniel there is a striking prophetic vision, given six centuries before Christ, of a ruler whose reign would arise out of the kingdoms which came after the empire of Alexander the Great:

> In the latter part of their reign, when rebels have become completely wicked, a fierce-looking king, a master of intrigue, will arise. He will become very strong, but not by his own power. He will cause astounding devastation and will succeed in whatever he does. He will destroy those who are mighty, the holy people. He will cause deceit to prosper, and he will consider himself superior. When they feel secure, he will destroy many and take his stand against the Prince of princes. **Yet he will be destroyed, but not by human power.** (Daniel 8:23-25)

The attributes of this ruler bear an uncanny resemblance to Muhammad's legacy, including Islam's sense of superiority; its orientation to success; use of deception; co-opting the strength and civilizational riches of others to enhance its own power; a knack of overcoming those who have been lulled into vulnerability by a false sense of security; and a track-record of devastating Christian and Jewish communities.

Could this prophecy refer to Muhammad and the religion which arose from the moral and spiritual wreckage of his life? If so, then the hope this scripture offers of eventual victory over the power of this 'king' also contains a warning, that victory will not be by 'human power'. To overcome this power, liberty will not be achieved simply through political, military or economic means.

Years of reflection and study have convinced me that this warning certainly holds true for Islam's claim to the right to dominate others. The power it claims is spiritual, and effective resistance, leading to lasting freedom from its claims to dominate, can only be achieved by spiritual means. Other forms of resistance may be necessary to manage the symptoms of Islamic hegemony, but they cannot address the root of the problem.

I am convinced that only the power of Christ and his cross provide the keys to lasting and conclusive release from Islam's demeaning claims. It is out of that conviction that I have written this book. Its purpose is to equip the saints to find freedom from the two aspects of Islam's strategy to dominate the human soul.

If you need to know more ...

This book is intended to be clear and straightforward. If the reader wishes to learn more about Islam, and to confirm this information from original sources, the research which underpins this book can be studied in greater detail in my earlier book *The Third Choice: Islam, Dhimmitude and Freedom*. That book has copious references to primary sources which document the claims made here about Islam.

CHAPTER 2

The *Shahada*

How to Become a Muslim

The word *Islam* is Arabic, meaning 'submission'. The word *Muslim* means a 'submitter', someone who surrenders to Allah.

What does this submission mean? The dominant picture of Allah in the Quran is the sovereign master, who has absolute authority over all things. The expected attitude to take towards this master is to submit to his authority.

Entering Islam means agreeing to submit to Allah and to the ways of his messenger. This is done by confessing the *shahada*, the Islamic creed:

> *Ashhadu an la ilaha illa Allah,*
> *wa ashhadu anna Muhammadun Rasulu Allah*

> 'I confess that there is no god but Allah,
> and I confess that Muhammad is Allah's Messenger.'

If you give the *shahada* your assent, and recite it for yourself, you have become a Muslim.

Although these are just a few words, their implications are vast. Reciting the *shahada* is a covenant declaration that Muhammad will be your guide for life. Being a Muslim – a 'submitter' – means following Muhammad as the unique, final messenger of Allah, who provides guidance for every particular of life.

The guidance of Muhammad is found in two sources, which together comprise the Islamic canon:

- The *Quran* is a book of revelations given to Muhammad from Allah.

- The *Sunna* is the example of Muhammad, which includes:

  > Teachings: the things Muhammad taught people to do.

  > Actions: the things Muhammad did.

The example of Muhammad is recorded for Muslims in two main formats. One is collections of *hadiths*, which are traditional sayings reporting things Muhammad did and said. Another format is the *siras*, which are biographies of Muhammad, and put his life in chronological order.

Muhammad's personality

Is Muhammad's example worth following? While some aspects of Muhammad's life are positive, others are admirable, and many are quite intriguing, even fascinating, there are episodes which are wrong by almost any ethical standard. Numerous statements and episodes in the *siras* and the *hadiths* are shocking, including acts of murder, torture, rape and other abuses of women, enslavement, theft, deception and incitement against non-Muslims.

Such material is not only disturbing as evidence of who Muhammad the individual was: it has implications for all Muslims. Muhammad's example was legislated by Allah in the Quran as the best model to follow, so such incidents can be – and have been – used as standards for Muslims to follow.

Moreover anyone who is bound by the *shahada* is obligated to follow Muhammad's example and to emulate his character. This follows from the *shahada*'s confession Muhammad is Allah's messenger. Reciting this means accepting Muhammad's guidance for your life.

In the Quran, Muhammad is called the best example, obligatory for all to follow:

> Whosoever obeys the Messenger, thereby obeys Allah ... (Q4:80)

> It is not for any believer, man or woman, when Allah and His Messenger have decreed a matter, to have the choice in the affair. Whosoever disobeys Allah and His Messenger has gone astray into manifest error. (Q33:36)

Those who follow Muhammad will be successful and blessed:

> Whoso obeys Allah and His Messenger, and fears Allah and has awe of Him, those – they are the triumphant. (Q24:52)

> Whosoever obeys Allah, and the Messenger – they are with those whom Allah has blessed ... (Q4:69)

Opposing Muhammad's instruction and example is disbelief. This leads to failure in this life and hellfire in the next. These curses are laid upon Muslims in the Quran:

But whoso makes a breach with the Messenger after the guidance has become clear to him, and follows a way other than the believers', him We shall turn over to what he has turned to and We shall roast him in hell – an evil homecoming! (Q4:115)

Whatever the Messenger gives you, take; whatever he forbids you, give over [i.e. abstain]. And fear Allah; surely Allah is terrible in retribution. (Q59:7)

And whoso rebels against Allah and His Messenger, for him there awaits the fire of Hell; therein they shall dwell forever. (Q72:23)

The Quran also commands fighting against anyone who rejects Muhammad:

Fight those who believe not in God and the Last Day and do not forbid what God and His Messenger have forbidden – such men as practice not the religion of truth, being of those who have been given the Book – until they pay the tribute out of hand and have been humbled. (Q9:29)

... so confirm the believers. I shall cast into the unbelievers' hearts terror; so smite above the necks, and smite every finger of them! That, because they had made a breach with Allah and with His Messenger; and whosoever makes a breach with Allah and with His Messenger, surely Allah is terrible in retribution. (Q8:12-13)

The Quran – Muhammad's personal document

Observant Muslims believe the Quran to be the letter-perfect revelation of Allah's guidance to humanity, delivered through his messenger Muhammad. If you accept the messenger, you must accept his message. The *shahada* therefore obligates a Muslim to believe in and obey the Quran.

A key thing to grasp about the manner of the Quran's production, is that Muhammad and the Quran are as intimately interconnected as a body is to its backbone. The *Sunna* is like the body and the Quran the backbone. Neither can stand without the other, and you cannot comprehend one without the other.

The Islamic *Sharia* – the 'way' to be a Muslim

To follow the teaching and example of Muhammad, a Muslim must look to the Quran and the *Sunna*. However this raw material is too complex and difficult for most Muslims to access, understand and use for themselves. It became obvious to religious leaders in the early Islamic centuries that the majority of Muslims must rely on an expert minority who could codify and organize the raw materials of Muhammad's *Sunna* and the Quran into a systematic and consistent set of rules for living. So, based on the Quran and the *Sunna* of Muhammad, Muslim jurists derived what came to be known as the *Sharia*, the 'path' or 'way' to live as a Muslim.

The Islamic *Sharia* can also be referred to as the *Sharia* of Muhammad, because it is based upon Muhammad's example and teaching. This system of rules defines a total way of life, both for the individual and the community. There can be no Islam without *Sharia*.

Because Muhammad's *Sunna* is the foundation of *Sharia* law, it is important not to relativize or gloss over the recorded details of what he did and said as recorded in the *hadiths* and the *sira*. Ignorance about Muhammad is ignorance about *Sharia*, and therefore about the human rights of people living under Islamic conditions. What Muhammad did, *Sharia* law commends to Muslims to emulate, and the lives of all are affected, both Muslims and non-Muslims. The relationship between Muhammad's life and the lives of people today may not always be a direct one, but it remains extremely powerful and significant.

Another thing to note about the *Sharia* is that, in contrast to the laws made by parliaments, which are devised by people and can be changed, the *Sharia* is thought to be divinely mandated, and therefore perfect and unchangeable. There are certain areas of flexibility – new circumstances keep arising so it is necessary for Muslim jurists to apply principles of reason and analogy to work out how the *Sharia* is to be applied – but these are adjustments around the margins of what is regarded as a pre-ordained, ideal system.

The promise of success

What then does Islam conceive to be the result of right guidance? For those who submit to Allah and accept his guidance, the intended result is **success** in this life and the next. The call of Islam is a call to success.

This call to success is proclaimed in the *adhan*, or call to worship *(salat)*, which sounds forth to Muslims five times a day:

Allah is Greater! Allah is Greater!
Allah is Greater! Allah is Greater!
I witness that there is no god but Allah.

I witness that there is no god but Allah.
I witness that Muhammad is the messenger of
Allah.
I witness that Muhammad is the messenger of
Allah.
Come to worship. Come to worship.
Come to success. Come to success.
Allah is Greater! Allah is Greater!
Allah is Greater! Allah is Greater!
There is no god but Allah.

The Quran emphasizes the importance of success a great deal. It divides humanity into winners and the rest. Those who do not accept Allah's guidance are repeatedly called 'the losers':

> Whoso desires another religion than Islam,
> it shall not be accepted of him;
> in the next world he shall be among **the losers**.
> (Q3:85)

> If thou associatest other gods with Allah,
> Thy work shall surely fail and thou wilt be among
> **the losers**. (Q39:65)

Islam's orientation to success and failure means that many Muslims have been schooled by their religion to regard themselves as superior to non-Muslims, and more pious Muslims are told they are superior to less pious Muslims, so discrimmination is a way of life in Islam.

A divided world

Throughout its chapters, the Quran has much to say, not only about Muslims, but about people of other faiths as well. Islamic legal terminology makes reference to four different types of people:

1. First and foremost there are the **genuine Muslims**.

2. Then there is another category called **hypocrites**, who are renegade Muslims.

3. The **'People of the Book'** are a subcategory of *mushrik*. This category includes Christians and Jews. They must be considered *mushrik*, because the Quran names both Christians and Jews as being guilty of *shirk* 'association'.

4. **Idolaters** were the dominant category amongst the Arabs before Muhammad appeared. The word for 'idolater' is *mushrik*, which literally means 'associater'. These are people who commit *shirk* 'association', which means saying that anyone or anything is like Allah.

The concept of 'People of the Book' signifies that Christianity and Judaism are related to and derived from Islam. Islam is regarded as the mother religion from which Christians and Jews had diverged over the centuries. According to the Quran, Christians and Jews follow a faith which was originally pure monotheism – in other words Islam – but their scriptures have been corrupted, and are no longer authentic. In this sense, Christianity and Judaism are regarded as distorted derivatives of Islam, and their followers have gone astray from the rightly guided path. Furthermore, Christians (and Jews) could not be freed from their ignorance until Muhammad came bringing the Quran (Q98:1). Muhammad was Allah's gift to Christians and Jews to correct misunderstandings. They should accept Muhammad as Allah's Messenger, and the Quran as his final revelation (Q5:15; Q57:28; Q4:47).

The Quran includes both positive and negative comments about Christians and Jews. In a positive light, it reports that some Christians and Jews are faithful and believe truly (Q3:113-14). However the same chapter says the test of their sincerity is that the genuine ones will become Muslims (Q3:199).

Although Jews and Christians are considered together in the one category of 'People of the Book', the Jews come off worse in the Quran. For example, the Quran says that it is Christians who will be 'nearest in love' to Muslims, but Jews and pagans will have the greatest enmity against Muslims. (Q5:82)

In the end, however, the Quran's final verdict is negative on both Jews and Christians alike. Condemnation is manifested in key theological claims, and incorporated into the daily prayers of every observant Muslim.

Daily prayers

The best-known chapter of the Quran is *al-Fatihah* 'The Opening'. This *sura* is recited as part of all the mandatory daily prayers – the *salat* –and repeated within each prayer. A faithful Muslim who said all their prayers would recite this *sura* at least seventeen times a day, and over five thousand times a year.

Al-Fatihah is a prayer for guidance:

> In the Name of Allah, the Merciful, the
> Compassionate
> Praise belongs to Allah, the Lord of all Being,
> the All-merciful, the All-compassionate,
> the Master of the Day of Doom.
> Thee only we serve; to Thee alone we pray for succor.
> Guide us in the straight path,

17

the path of those whom Thou hast blessed,
not of **those against whom Thou art wrathful,**
nor of **those who are astray.**

This is a prayer asking Allah's help to lead the believer along the 'straight path'. As such it is true to the heart of Islam's message of guidance.

But who are those who are said to have earned Allah's wrath, or gone astray from the straight path? Who are these people who deserve to be stigmatized in every Muslim's prayers, each day, hundreds of thousands of times in many Muslims' lifetimes?

Muhammad clarified the meaning of this *sura*, saying 'Those who have earned the anger are the Jews and those who are led astray are the Christians.

It is remarkable that the daily prayers of every Muslim, at the very core of Islam, include a rejection of Christians and Jews as misguided and objects of Allah's wrath.

Theological claims about non-Muslims

Moving beyond solemn ritual, the Quran and *Sunna* teach that:

1. Christians and Jews who cling to their *shirk* and continue to disbelieve in Muhammad and his monotheism – i.e. those who do not convert to Islam – will go to hell.

2. Muslims are superior to other peoples – 'the best people' – and their role is to instruct them concerning what is right and wrong, commanding what is honorable, and forbidding what is shameful. (Q3:110)

3. Islam's destiny is to rule over all other religions. (Q48:28)

4. To achieve this ascendancy, Muslims are to fight against Jews and Christians (the Peoples of the Book) until they are defeated and humbled, and forced to pay tribute to the Muslim community. (Q9:29)

5. In the end-times Judaism and Christianity will be destroyed. Muhammad taught that when Isa, the Islamic Jesus returns to the earth, he will destroy Christianity ('break the Cross'), and make an end of the legal tolerance of Christians to live under Islamic rule ('there will be no *jizya*'). Scholars interpret this *hadith* to mean that Isa the Muslim prophet (i.e. Jesus) will force all Christians, and followers of all other faiths, to convert to Islam at the point of the sword.

6. In addition to all this, there are numerous specific theological claims about the Jews. For example, Muhammad taught that at the end, the very stones will lend their voices to help Muslims kill the Jews.

Lawful deception

One of the more problematic aspects of the Islamic *sharia* is its teachings on lying and deception. While it must be acknowledged that lying is considered a very serious sin in Islam, there are situations where lying is permissible, according to Islamic authorities, based upon Muhammad's example. There are several distinct circumstances where Muslims are permitted or required to lie. For example, a chapter in the *Sahih al-Bukhari* is

19

headed 'He who makes peace between people is not a liar.' According to this aspect of Muhammad's example, one of the circumstances in which Muslims are permitted to say untrue things is when reconciling people will have a positive effect.

Another context for lawful lying is when Muslims are in danger from non-Muslims (Q3:28). From this verse is derived the concept of *taqiyya*, which refers to the practice of deception in order to keep Muslims safe.

The consensus of Muslim scholars has been that Muslims, when living under the political dominance of non-Muslims, are allowed to show friendliness and kindness to non-Muslims as a protective measure, so long as they hold fast to their faith (and enmity) in their hearts.

One implication of this doctrine is that observant Muslims' behavior towards non-Muslims might be expected to become less friendly, and their beliefs less veiled, as their political power increases.

Other circumstances where *sharia* law encourages Muslims to lie include: between husbands and wives to maintain marital harmony; when resolving disputes; when telling the truth might cause you to incriminate yourself; when someone has entrusted you with their secret; and in warfare.

More generally, Islam advocates an ethic for lying in which the end justifies the means. Some scholars have made fine distinctions between different kinds of lies, for example, giving a misleading impression is preferred to telling a plain lie.

An ethically damaged community

A utilitarian ethic for lying and truth-telling can be very damaging. It destroys trust and creates confusion, damaging domestic and political cultures. If husbands habitually lie to their wives to 'smooth over differences', then this will erode trust within marriage. On a societal level, a culture of lawful deception causes a breakdown of trust. This means that conducting business is more expensive, conflicts are prolonged, and reconciliation is much harder to achieve.

When someone leaves Islam, it is important that they specifically renounce this aspect of Muhammad's example.

Think for yourself

Because of the way knowledge is organized and even guarded in Islam, it can be difficult to know what Islam 'really' teaches on certain subjects.

The primary sources of Islam are large and complex, and the process of deriving *Sharia* rulings from the source materials of the Quran and the *Sunna* is considered to be a highly skilled one, requiring long years of training, which the vast majority of Muslims are not able to undertake. This means that, from a practical point of view, it is expedient for Muslims to rely on their scholars for guidance in matters of faith. Indeed Islamic jurisprudence instructs Muslims to seek out and follow someone who is more knowledgeable about matters of faith than themselves, and to follow that person. If Muslims have questions about *Sharia* law, they are supposed to ask someone who has the required expertise.

Islamic religious knowledge is not democratized in the way Biblical knowledge has been in recent centuries. In Islam certain things are just not discussed if there is no need to mention them, or it might put Islam in a bad light to do so: information about Islam is made available on a need-to-know basis.

No-one should let themselves be intimidated by claims that they have no right to express opinions about Islam, the Quran, or the *Sunna* of Muhammad. In this age, when primary source material is easily available on these subjects, everyone – Christians, Jews, atheists or Muslims – should take every opportunity to inform themselves, and speak out their views on these matters. Anyone and everyone who is affected by Islam has the right to inform themselves and form their own opinions about it.

CHAPTER 3

The *Dhimma* Pact

The Three Choices

In 2006, when Pope Benedict gave his now famous Regensburg lecture, he quoted Emperor Manuel II Paleologus, who spoke of Muhammad's 'command to spread by the sword the faith he preached.'

The pope's comments elicited a sharp reaction from Muslims all over the world. One of the most interesting responses was from Sheikh 'Abdul Aziz al-Sheikh, Grand Mufti of Saudi Arabia, who issued a press release stating that Islam was not spread by violence. He argued that it is wrong to accuse Islam of this, because infidels had a third choice. The first option was Islam, the second the sword, but the third was, as he put it, to:

> 'surrender and pay tax, and they will be allowed to remain in their land, observing their religion under the protection of Muslims.'

The Grand Mufti referred his readers to the example of Muhammad. He said 'Those who read the Quran and

23

Sunnah can understand the facts.' The three choices the mufti referred to were:

i) convert to Islam;

ii) the sword – kill or be killed; or

iii) surrender to the forces of Islam.

The first two choices go back to Muhammad, who said:

> I have been ordered (by Allah) to fight against the people until they testify that none has the right to be worshipped but Allah and that Muhammad is the Messenger of Allah, ... so if they perform all that, then they save their lives and property from me ...

However this was moderated by other statements in which Muhammad gave an additional option, in addition to Islam or the sword, which was to surrender, and pay the *jizya* tribute:

> Fight in the name of Allah and in the way of Allah. Fight against those who disbelieve in Allah. Make a holy war ...
> **When you meet your enemies who are polytheists, invite them to three courses of action.**
> If they respond to any one of these, you also accept it and withhold yourself from doing them any harm.
> Invite them to (accept) Islam;
> if they respond to you, accept it from them
> and desist from fighting against them ....
> If they refuse to accept Islam, demand from them the *jizya*.
> If they agree to pay, accept it from them and hold off your hands.
> If they refuse to pay the tax, seek Allah's help and fight them.

In *The Third Choice* what the Grand Mufti called the 'facts' found in the Quran and the *Sunna* are explained, in accordance with the interpretations of great Islamic commentators, and lived out by non-Muslims under Sharia law, down through history.

Communities which surrendered to Islamic rule are considered by Islamic law to have accepted a *dhimma* pact, which is a covenant of surrender in which the non-Muslim community agrees to pay annual tribute to the Muslims, and adopts an attitude of defeated humility. In return the non-Muslims are allowed to keep the faith which they had before conquest. Non-Muslims who live under these conditions are known as *dhimmis*.

The *dhimma* system is a political manifestation of two principles based on the Quran: i) that Islam should triumph over other religions (Q48:28), and ii) that Muslims must be in a position of power to enforce Islam's teaching on what is right and wrong (Q3:110).

The jizya payment rituals

In Islamic law – Sharia law – the *dhimma* pact treats non-Muslims as people whose lives would have been forfeit, if Muslims had not spared them. This goes back to a pre-Islamic idea that if you conquered someone, and let them live, they owed you their head. Because of this, the annual *jizya* head tax, paid by adult *dhimmi* males to the Islamic state, is described in authoritative Islamic sources as a redemption paid by dhimmis in return for their blood. Muslim lexicographers defined *jizya* as:

> ... the tax that is taken from the free non-Muslim of a Muslim government whereby they ratify the compact [the *dhimma* pact] that ensures them protection, **as**

though it were a compensation for their not being slain. (Lane's *Arabic-English Lexicon*)

At-Fayyish, a 19ᵗʰ Century Algerian commentator, explained this principle in his commentary of Q9:29:

> "It was said: it [*jizya*] is a satisfaction for their blood. It is said 'X' has sufficed ... to compensate for their not being slain. Its purpose is to substitute for the duties (*wajib*) of killing and of slavery.... It is for the benefit of Muslims."

Or, as William Eton explained more than a century earlier in his compendious *Survey of the Turkish Empire*, published in 1799:

> The very words of their formulary, given to the Christian subjects on their paying the capitation tax [*jizya*], import, that the sum of money received, is taken as compensation for being permitted to wear their heads that year.

In *The Third Choice* the powerful symbolism of the annual *jizya* tax payment ritual is explained. *Dhimmi* males were required to undergo this ritual all over the Muslim world until modern times. It involved one or two blows on the neck, and in many versions, a form of ritual strangulation, signifying that the *dhimmi* is paying for his very life with this tax. The ritual was an enactment of the death from which the *jizya* payment won an annual reprieve. *The Third Choice* provides dozens of references to this ritual of decapitation, from Morocco to Bukhara, from the 9th to the 20th centuries, taken from both Muslim and non-Muslim sources. The ritual continued in some Muslim countries, such as Yemen and Afghanistan, right up until the exodus of Jews to Israel in the late 1940's and early

1950's, and in recent years there have been many calls for it to be brought back.

In essence, non-Muslims are regarded in classical Islamic law as people who owe their lives to their Muslim conquerors. They are expected to adopt an attitude of gratitude and humble inferiority: Islamic commentators are quite explicit on this issue.

Many sharia regulations were designed to impose inferiority and vulnerability upon non-Muslims. For example:

- The witness of *dhimmi*s is not accepted in Sharia courts: this made them vulnerable to all kinds of oppression;

- *Dhimmi* houses had to be lower than Muslim houses;

- *Dhimmi*s were not allowed to ride horses or raise their heads above those of Muslims;

- *Dhimmi*s were allowed no means of self-defence, which made them vulnerable to acts of violence at the hands of Muslims;

- No public display of religious symbols or rituals were permitted;

- No criticism of Islam was permitted;

- *Dhimmi*s had to dress differently: the colored patch was an Islamic invention.

- There were also many other laws which enforced humiliation and segregation on non-Muslim communities.

Such laws were understood as a social and legal expression of being made 'small', as commanded by the Quran (9:29).

The *dhimma* system was designed to reduce and demean the non-Muslim communities it dominated. The 18th century Moroccan commentator Ibn 'Ajibah described its purpose – in a passage unearthed, translated, and published for the first time in *The Third Choice* – as a killing of the soul:

> [The *dhimmi*] is commanded to put his soul, good fortune and desires to death. Above all he should kill the love of life, leadership and honor. [The *dhimmi*] is to invert the longings of his soul, he is to load it down more heavily than it can bear until it is completely submissive. Thereafter nothing will be unbearable for him. He will be indifferent to subjugation or might. Poverty and wealth will be the same to him; praise and insult will be the same; preventing and yielding will be the same; lost and found will be the same. Then, when all things are the same, it [the soul] will be submissive and yield willingly what it should give.

In Islamic law, a severe penalty applied for non-compliance with the *dhimma* pact. If a *dhimmi* omitted to pay the *jizya* tax, or failed to obey the regulations imposed upon *dhimmi*s, the penalty was that *jihad* started again. This meant war conditions: the *dhimmis'* possessions were to be looted, their women enslaved and raped, and the men killed (or converted at the point of the sword).

A famous example of a *dhimma* pact, known as the Pact of Umar, includes a clause where the Christians invoke this penalty upon themselves:

> These are the conditions that we set against ourselves and followers of our religion in return for safety and protection. If we break any of these promises that we set for your benefit against ourselves, then our

Dhimmah is broken and you are allowed to do with us what you are allowed of people of defiance and rebellion.

The same point is made by Ibn Qudama, that in case of non-compliance with the *dhimma* pact, the *dhimmi*'s life and possessions are forfeit:

A protected person who violates his protection agreement, whether by refusing to pay the head tax [*jizya*] or to submit to the laws of the community ... makes his person and his goods 'licit' [*halal* – freely available to be killed or captured by Muslims].

As a ritualized enactment of one's own decapitation, the *jizya* payment can be considered to be a 'blood pact' or 'blood oath', in which the participant invokes death against themselves by simulating the manner of their execution, should they ever fail to keep the conditions of their pact. Such oaths have been used for centuries in initiation ceremonies by secret societies and occult groups, for they are recognized to have psycho-spiritual power to bind initiates to submission and obedience.

The *jizya* ritual symbolically demands the consent of the *dhimmi* who participates in it to forfeit his very head if he violates any of the terms of the *dhimma* covenant, which has spared his life. It is an act of self-cursing, which says in effect 'You can rightfully have my head if I break any of the conditions of my covenant.' Later, if a *dhimmi* violates his covenant, he has already pronounced the death penalty against himself, by virtue of undergoing this public ritual, and if he is killed, it would be by his own prior permission.

In *The Third Choice* numerous examples are given of when *dhimmi* communities have had to endure *jihad* conditions as a result of a breach of their *dhimma*, whether real or perceived. The history of many *dhimmi* communities has been marked by a series of traumatic historical milestones involving massacres, rape and looting, which have served to keep the non-Muslims in a state of perpetual intimidation, and have helped reinforce the psychological and spiritual bondage of the *dhimma* over the whole community.

Dhimmitude

The term *dhimmitude* is used to describe the totality of conditions which a *dhimma* covenant produces. Like sexism and racism, dhimmitude is not only expressed in legal and social structures, but in a psychology of inferiority, and a will to serve, which the dominated community adopts in an attempt at self-preservation. As the great medieval Jewish scholar Maimonides put it, 'We have acquiesced, both old and young, to inure ourselves to humiliation ...', and early in the 20th century, Jovan Cvijic described how the intergenerational fear of violence from the ruling Turks and Muslim Albanians produced typical adaptive psychological responses among the Christian populations of the Balkans:

> [they became] ... accustomed to belonging to an inferior, servile class, whose duty it is to make themselves acceptable to the master, to humble themselves before him and to please him. These people become close-mouthed, secretive, cunning; they lose all confidence in others; they grow used to hypocrisy and meanness because these are necessary in order for them to live and to avoid violent punishments.

The direct influence of oppression and violence is manifested in almost all the Christians as feelings of fear and apprehension. ... In Macedonia I heard people say: 'Even in our dreams we flee from the Turks and the Albanians.'

Matching the inferiority of the *dhimmi* is the superiority of the Muslim, who is afforded a sense of being generous, having granted the *dhimmi* quarter, and refrained from taking his possessions. As one Iranian convert to Christianity put it 'Christianity is still viewed as the religion of an inferior class of people. Islam is the religion of masters and rulers, Christianity is the religion of slaves.'

This worldview of dhimmitude is as pernicious for Muslims as it is humiliating for non-Muslims. Muslims injure themselves when they establish circumstances where they have no possibility of learning to compete on an even footing. Just as economic protectionism can cause the competitive ability of a whole nation to atrophy, so the 'religious protectionism' of the *dhimma* can mean that Muslims come to rely upon a false sense of superiority, which ultimately weakens them, and damages their ability to gain a true understanding of themselves and the world around them.

The system of dhimmitude engenders a set of deeply ingrained attitudes on both sides from generation to generation. Just as racism continues in America and other nations more than a century after race-based slavery was abolished, so the institution of dhimmitude continues to affect, indeed to dominate, relationships between Muslims and others, even when the *jizya* tax is but a distant memory. The dynamics can even extend to affect interfaith relations involving minority immigrant

Muslim communities, in societies which have never been subject to the *Sharia*.

The Dhimmitude of the West

One of the points made in *The Third Choice* is that, in a sustained process of ideological subversion, Western nations are increasingly coming under the world view of dhimmitude. This is manifested, for example, in the long line-up of Western leaders who have praised Islam, and declared it to be a religion of peace, whilst at the same time expressing gratitude to Islam.

A notable example was President Obama's 2009 Cairo speech, in which he spoke civilization's 'debt to Islam'. Just as the *dhimmi* is meant to feel that he owes his life to his conquerors so the 'civilization' of dhimmitude is supposed to feel indebted to Islam.

The world view of dhimmitude is also manifested in a persistent pattern of denial about the historical and theological realities of the *dhimma* as an integral part of Islam, and a dominant feature of the history of conquered peoples living under Islam. This denial is crippling academic inquiry and political discourse.

The dhimmitude of the West is not a new phenomenon. Much of Europe has suffered from *jihad* in the not too distant past. The coastlines of France, Italy, Spain, Ireland and England, were plagued by *jihadi* pirates – Barbary corsairs – right up until the early 19th century. Historians have estimated that hundreds of thousands of Europeans were abducted by the corsairs and sold into the slave markets of the Barbary coast from the 11th to the 19th centuries. Until the French annexed Algeria in 1830, European nations and the United States were paying large tributes (considered a form of *jizya* in Islamic law) to the Barbary states in order to limit the trade in European slaves.

Although fear of *jihad* terror is, for Europeans, not a new phenomenon, undoubtedly the recent rise in *jihad* terrorist attacks is a significant contributor to the intimidation and encroaching dhimmitude of the West.

Religious persecution and the dhimma's return

During the 19th and 20th centuries various European powers forced the Muslim world to downgrade or dismantle the *dhimma* system. However in recent decades the regulations and world view of the *dhimma* has been returning all across the Muslim world, and with it an increasing climate of prejudice, intimidation and religious discrimination. When the West turns a blind eye to the plight of Christians in Pakistan, Iraq or Egypt, they are helping to conceal the reality of dhimmitude and its growing influence on world affairs.

CHAPTER 4

Muhammad and Rejection

Muhammad is the root and the body of Islam. This chapter gives an overview of some features of Muhammad's life story which lie behind the *dhimma* pact and the principles of Islam.

A painful start

Muhammad was born in c. 570 AD, into the Quraish, an Arab tribe in Mecca. His father, 'Abdullah bin 'Abd al-Muttalib, died before Muhammad was born. He was then fostered out to another family to be cared for in his early years. His mother died when he was six, and his powerful grandfather looked after him for a while, but then he too passed away when Muhammad was eight. So Muhammad went to live with his father's brother Abu Talib, where he was given the humble task of looking after his uncle's camels and sheep. Later he was to state: 'There is no prophet but has shepherded a flock', turning his lowly role into a mark of distinction.

Although some of Muhammad's other uncles were wealthy, it seems they did nothing to help him. The Quran expresses contempt for one uncle, nicknamed *Abu Lahab* 'father of flame': he would burn in hell, because of his contempt for Muhammad:

> Perish the hands of Abu Lahab, and perish he;
> his wealth avails him not, neither what he has earned;
> he shall roast at a flaming fire
> and his wife, the carrier of the firewood,
> upon her neck a rope of palm-fibre. (Q111)

An unequal marriage

As a young man, Muhammad was twenty-five, and in Khadijah's employ, when she proposed marriage to him. She was the older of the two. Khadijah feared that her father would reject the marriage, so she had him marry them while he was drunk. When he came to his senses the father was furious to discover what had happened.

In Arabian culture, a man had to pay a bride price for a bride, after which she was considered a chattel, even to the extent that a wife formed part of his estate, and his male heir could marry her if he wished. In contrast to the usual situation, Khadijah was powerful and wealthy – Muhammad's biographer Ibn Ishaq calls her a woman 'of dignity and wealth' – and Muhammad was poor with few prospects. Khadijah had also been married twice before. The contrast between the usual understanding of marriage and the arrangement between Khadijah and Muhammad is striking.

A bereaved parent

Khadijah and Muhammad were to have six (by some accounts seven) children together. Altogether Muhammad had three (or four) sons, but they all died young, leaving him no male heirs. This was no doubt another source of disappointment in Muhammad's experience of family life.

Painful experiences of family life

In conclusion, in Muhammad's family circumstances there were several potentially painful features, including being orphaned and losing his grandfather, becoming a poor dependent relation, having to be married by a drunk father-in-law, and becoming the target of hostility from powerful relatives. The great exceptions to this pattern of rejection were the care shown to him by his uncle Abu Talib, and Khadijah's choice of him as a marriage partner, which rescued him from poverty.

A new religion is founded

When Muhammad was around forty years old, he began to experience visitations from a spirit which he later identified as the angel Jibril (Gabriel of the Bible).

Self-rejection

Muhammad became extremely distressed at these visitations, and wondered whether he was possessed. He even contemplated suicide, saying, 'I will go to the top of the mountain and throw myself down that I may kill myself and gain rest.' His wife Khadijah comforted him in his great anxiety and took him to her cousin, Waraqa, a Christian, who announced that he was a prophet, and no madman.

Later, when the revelations ceased for a time, Muhammad was again beset with suicidal thoughts, but each time he was about to throw himself off a mountain, Jibril would appear and reassure him: 'O Muhammad! You are indeed Allah's Messenger in truth.'

It seems Muhammad feared being rejected as a fraud, for in one of the early *suras* Allah assures Muhammad that he had not and would not disown him (Q93).

The Muslim community grew slowly at first, Khadijah becoming the first convert. The next was Muhammad's young cousin 'Ali, who had been brought up in Muhammad's own house. Others followed, mainly from among the poor, slaves or freed slaves.

Muhammad's own tribe

At first the new religion was kept secret by its followers, but after three years Muhammad received word from Allah to make it public. He did this by convening a family conference at which he invited his relatives into Islam.

At first Muhammad's fellow Quraysh tribespeople of Mecca were disposed to listen to him, but only until he began to disparage their gods. After this the Muslims became what Ibn Ishaq called 'a despised minority'. Tensions ran high, and the two sides came to blows.

As opposition mounted, Muhammad's uncle Abu Talib protected him. When others in Mecca approached saying 'O Abu Talib, your nephew has cursed our gods, insulted our religion, mocked our way of life … either you must stop him or you must let us get at him ...', Abu Talib put them off.

The disbelieving Arabs instituted an economic and social boycott against Muhammad's clan, forbidding commerce and intermarriage with them. Because of their poverty, the Muslims were vulnerable. Ibn Ishaq summarizes their treatment at the hands of the Quraysh:

> Then the Quraysh showed their enmity to all those who followed the apostle; every clan which contained Muslims attacked them, imprisoning them, and beating them, allowing them no food or drink, and exposing them to the burning heat of Mecca, so as to seduce them from their religion. Some gave way under pressure of persecution, and others resisted them, being protected by God.

Muhammad's own person did not escape the dangers and insults: he had dirt thrown over him, and even animal intestines when he was praying.

When the persecutions did not let up, eighty-three Muslim men and their families emigrated to Christian Abyssinia for refuge, where they found protection.

Self-doubt

At one point Muhammad appeared to waver in his monotheism, under pressure from the Quraysh. They had offered to him a deal whereby they would worship Allah if he worshipped their gods. This he would not accept, receiving the verses of Q109:6 'To you your religion, to me my religion!' However Muhammad must have hesitated, for al-Tabari records that as he was receiving Q53, there were 'revealed' to him what came to be known as a 'Satanic verse' in reference to the Meccan goddesses al-Lat, al-Uzza and Manat: 'these are the exalted *gharaniq* (cranes) whose intercession is approved'.

When they heard this verse, the heathen Quraysh were delighted and began to worship with the Muslims. However the angel Jibril rebuked Muhammad: the verse was abrogated and said to have come from Satan. Muhammad then made it known that the verse had been withdrawn, but this attracted even more scorn from the Quraysh, who became even more hostile to Muhammad and his followers.

After this, Muhammad received the verse (Q22:52) which claimed that all prophets before him had also been led astray. Here again we see Muhammad taking a potential cause for shame, and turning it into a mark of distinction.

In the face of mockery and charges that he was a faker, which stung him deeply, Muhammad received verses from Allah, validating him, and stating that his character was remarkable, he was not in error, but a man of integrity (Q68:1-4; 53:1-3).

A variety of traditions also report that Muhammad came to believe in the superiority of his race, tribe, clan and parentage. In response to claims of illegitimacy, he said that all his ancestors were born in, and none out of wedlock, all the way back to Adam: he was the best man, from the best clan (the Hashemites) of the best nation (the Arabs). He said 'I am the best of you in spirit and the best of you in parentage. ... I am the choicest of the chosen; so whoever loves the Arabs, it is through loving me that he loves them.'

More experiences of rejection

Things had not been going well for some time when Muhammad lost both his wife Khadijah and his uncle Abu Talib in the same year. These were huge blows. Without their support and protection, the Quraysh were emboldened to be even more hostile against him.

Arab society was based around alliances and client relationships. The way to find security was to come under the protection of someone more powerful than yourself. With dangers to him and his followers increasing, and having been rejected by his own tribe, Muhammad went out to seek alternative protectors elsewhere. He was mocked and ridiculed, and at Ta'if was chased away by a mob.

Things were not looking good for Muhammad. Yet eventually he did manage to find a community who was willing to protect him. These were Arabs from Yathrib (later called Medina), a city where many Jews also lived.

New allies and flight from Mecca

During an annual fair at Mecca, a group of visitors from Medina pledged loyalty and obedience to Muhammad, agreeing to live by his message of monotheism.

In this first pledge no commitment to fight was made. However at the next year's fair a larger group of Medinans pledged the protection which Muhammad had been seeking. The Medinans, who came to be known as *Ansar*, or 'helpers', undertook to wage 'war in complete obedience to the apostle'.

After this, a decision was taken for the Muslims to migrate to Medina to form a political safe-haven.

Muhammad was the last to flee Mecca, escaping in the middle of the night through a back window. When they arrived in Medina, Muhammad was able to proclaim his message unhindered, and virtually all the Medinan Arabs converted to Islam within the first year. Muhammad was by this time just over fifty-two years old.

During the Meccan years, Muhammad was rejected by his own family, and tribe. With few exceptions, only the humble poor believed in him, and he was mocked, threatened, humiliated and attacked by all the rest.

Muhammad had been very unsure of himself at first, fearing rejection of his sense of prophetic calling. At one point he even seemed to accept the Quraysh's gods. However, in the end, despite all the opposition, Muhammad acted with determined perseverance and acquired a group of dedicated followers.

Rejection and the Meccan revelations

Peaceful witness?

Many writers have claimed that Muhammad's decade of witness in Mecca was peaceful. In one sense this was true. However, although no physical violence is commanded in the Meccan chapters of the Quran, it was certainly contemplated, and the early revelations denounce Muhammad's neighbors in terrifying language, announcing dire torments for rejecters in the hereafter.

One of the functions of the Meccan judgment verses in the Quran was to vindicate Muhammad in the face of rejection from the Quraysh Arabs. For example, Muhammad says that those who laughed at the Muslims will get their comeuppance. The believers, sitting back drinking wine in luxury on their couches in paradise, will laugh when they gaze down at the unbelievers roasting in hellfire (Q83:29-36).

These judgement messages undoubtedly stoked the fires of conflict in Mecca. The pagans did not like what they were hearing.

Forewarned in Mecca

Not only did Muhammad preach eternal judgment, Ibn Ishaq records that it was early in the Meccan period that Muhammad first foreshadowed his intention to kill the pagans: 'Will you listen to me, O Quraysh? By Him who holds my life in His hand, I bring you slaughter.'

Later, just before Muhammad fled to Medina, a group of Quraysh came to him and confronted him with the charge that he was threatening to kill those who rejected him: 'Muhammad alleges that ... if you do not follow him you will be slaughtered, and when you are raised from the dead you will be burned in the fire of hell.' Muhammad confessed this was correct: 'I do say that.'

Out of the crucible of rejection and persecution in Medina came the Muslim community's resolve – confirmed by divine mandate – to go to war against their opponents.

Winners and losers

The Islamic concept of success and the language of winners and losers first begin to emerge as themes in the *suras* of the Quran in the middle of Muhammad's thirteen years in Mecca. Around this time, in repeated references to the conflicts between Moses and the Egyptian idolaters, the Quran describes the outcomes in terms of winners and losers (e.g. Q20:64,69; Q26:40-44; Q29:39).

However it is only towards the end of the Meccan period that Muhammad applies the terminology of success to the struggle between himself and his opponents. In the tenth sura, from the period just before the migration to Medina, Muhammad declares that those who reject Allah's revelations will be losers (Q10:95).

Muhammad's *fitna* worldview

The Arabic word *fitna* 'trial, persecution, temptation' is of crucial importance in understanding Muhammad's metamorphosis into a military leader. The word is derived from *fatana* 'to turn away from, to tempt, seduce or subject to trials'. Its base meaning is to prove a metal by fire. *Fitna* can include either temptation or trial, including both positive and negative inducements, up to and including torture. It could encompass seducing someone, or tearing them limb from limb.

Fitna became a key concept in theological reflection upon the early Muslim community's experiences with unbelievers. Muhammad's charge against the Quraysh was that they used *fitna* – including insult, slander, torture, exclusion, economic pressures, and other inducements – in order to get them to leave Islam or to dilute its claims.

The first verses revealed concerning fighting made clear that **the whole purpose** of fighting and killing was to eliminate *fitna*:

> And fight in the way of Allah with those who fight with you,
> but aggress not: Allah loves not the aggressors.
> And slay them wherever you come upon them,
> and expel them from where they expelled you;
> **persecution (*fitna*) is more grievous than slaying**

....
Fight them, til there is no persecution (*fitna*);
and the religion is Allah's; then if they give over [i.e.
cease their disbelief and opposition to Islam],
there shall be no enmity save for evildoers.
(Q2:190-93)

The idea that *fitna* of Muslims was 'more grievous than slaying' proved to be a significant one. The same phrase would be revealed again after an attack on a Meccan caravan (Q2:217) during the sacred month (a period during which Arab tribal traditions prohibited raiding). It implied, at the very least, that shedding the blood of infidels is a lesser thing than a Muslim being led astray from their faith.

The other significant phrase in this passage from Q2 is 'fight them until there is no *fitna*'. This too was revealed a second time, after the battle of Badr, during the second year in Medina (Q8:39).

These *fitna* phrases, each revealed twice, established the principle that *jihad* was justified by the existence of any obstacle to people entering Islam, or of inducements to Muslims to abandon their faith. However grievous it might be to fight and kill others, undermining or obstructing Islam was worse.

Most Muslim scholars extended the concept of *fitna* to include even the mere existence of unbelief, so the phrase could be interpreted as 'unbelief is worse than killing'

Understood this way, the phrase '*fitna* is worse than killing' became a universal mandate to fight and kill all infidels who rejected Muhammad's message, whether they were interfering with Muslims or not. Merely for unbelievers to 'commit disbelief' – to use a phrase of

45

the great commentator Ibn Kathir – was a greater evil than their being killed. This provided the justification for warfare to eliminate disbelief, and make Islam dominant over all other religions (Q2:193; 8:39).'

Implications for non-Muslims

The root of the rejection of non-believers in Islamic law is found in Muhammad's emotional worldview and his own responses to rejection.

Initially Muhammad focussed his enmity on his fellow tribes people, the pagan Arabs. We can observe a trend in Muhammad's treatment of the pagan Arabs whereby a sense of offense at the trials they heaped upon the Muslims is used to justify the doctrine that the very existence of disbelief constitutes *fitna*. The same trend also is found in Muhammad's dealings with the People of the Book. As rejecters of Islam, they become permanently marked as guilty, and deserving to be subjugated and treated as inferior.

Other rejection reactions

In the story of Muhammad's prophetic career, we have observed a range of responses to rejection.[1] Early on Muhammad shows self-rejecting reactions, including suicidal thoughts, fear that he was possessed, and despair.

There are also self-validating reactions, as if to counter the fear of rejection. These include assertions that Allah would punish his enemies in hell; claims to cover points of potential embarrassment, such as the assertion that

---

1 For a discussion of responses to rejection, see Noel and Phyl Gibson, 1987, *Evicting Demonic Squatters and Breaking Bondages.'*

all prophets had been led astray at some point by Satan; and verses sent down from Allah which declared that those who followed Muhammad's revelations would be winners in this life and the next.

Finally, aggressive responses came to dominate. These result in the doctrine of *jihad* to eliminate *fitna* by fighting against and conquering non-Muslims.

Retribution

As Muhammad's military strength in Medina grew, and victories began to come, his treatment of defeated enemies said much about his motivations for fighting. A telling incident was Muhammad's treatment of 'Uqba, who had earlier thrown camel dung and intestines on him. 'Uqba was captured in the battle of Badr, and pleaded for his life saying 'But who will look after my children, O Muhammad?' The answer was 'Hell!', and then Muhammad had 'Uqba killed. After the battle of Badr, the bodies of the killed Meccans were thrown into a pit, and Muhammad went to the pit in the middle of the night to mock the Meccan dead.

Such incidents show that Muhammad sought retribution and vindication against those who had rejected him. He insisted on having the last word, even to the dead.

The conquest of Mecca

Those who rejected Muhammad were always at the top of his assassination list. When he conquered Mecca, Muhammad discouraged slaughter. However there was a small hit-list of people to be killed under all circumstances. Three were apostates, two (one a woman) were people who had insulted Muhammad in Mecca, and two were slave girls who used to sing satirical songs about him.

The Meccan hit-list reflects Muhammad's revulsion of being rejected. The apostates embodied the threat of *fitna*, for they were witness to the possibility of leaving Islam, while those who mocked or insulted Muhammad were dangerous because they had the power to undermine the faith of others.

The treaty of Hudaybiyyah

Before the conquest of Mecca, Muhammad had a vision in which he performed a pilgrimage to Mecca. This was impossible at the time, as the Muslims were in a state of war with the Meccans. After his vision, Muhammad negotiated a treaty which allowed him to make his pilgrimage. The treaty was to be for ten years, and one of its stipulations was that Muhammad would return to the Meccans anyone who came to him without the permission of their guardian. This would include slaves and women. The treaty also allowed people from either side to enter into alliances with each other.

Muhammad, for his part, did not keep his side of the treaty, because when people came to him from Mecca to reclaim their wives or slaves, he would refuse to return the fugitives, citing the authority of Allah. The first case was a woman, Umm Kulthum, whose brothers came to retrieve her. Muhammad refused, for, as Ibn Ishaq put it, 'Allah forbade it' (Q60:10).

Q60 instructs the Muslims not to take unbelievers as their friends. It says that if any Muslims secretly love the Meccans, they have gone astray: in any case, the unbelievers' desire is only to cause the Muslims to disbelieve. The whole Q60 is in conflict with the spirit of the treaty of Hudaybiyyah, which had stated 'We will not show enmity one to another and there shall be no secret reservation or bad faith.' However later, when the Muslims attacked and conquered Mecca, this was said to be justified on the basis that it was the Quraysh who violated the treaty.

After this, Allah declared that no more treaties could be made with idolaters – 'Allah is quit … of the idolaters' and 'slay the idolaters wherever you find them' (Q9:3-5).

This sequence of events illustrates what became an entrenched Islamic perspective, that non-Muslim disbelievers were by nature pact breakers, unable to keep covenants (Q9:2-8). At the same time, Muhammad, under instruction from Allah, claimed his right to break pacts with infidels. When Muhammad, claiming the authority of a higher power, violated his agreements, this was not regarded as unrighteous.

Such incidents as these reveal that Muhammad, by consigning unbelievers to the category of those who would seduce Muslims from their faith (i.e. they would commit *fitna*) made it impossible to have normal relationships with them, as long as they refused to accept Islam.

Striving against the Jews

Muhammad's interactions with the Jews of Medina and Khaybar form the foundation for the later development of the *dhimma* pact system for 'People of the Book'.

Muhammad's initial views on the Jews

During the Meccan period, the primary interest which Muhammad had with Jews concerned his claim that he was a prophet in a long line which included many Jewish prophets. In the Meccan *suras*, and the revelations from the first months in Medina, there are numerous references to Jews. When the Meccan Quran referred to the Jews, it was to make the point that although some of them were believing, and some were not, Muhammad's message would come as a blessing to them (Q98:1-8).

Muhammad had also encountered some Christians in his time in Mecca, and these contacts had been encouraging. Khadijah's Christian cousin, Waraqa had identified Muhammad as a prophet, and Abyssinian Christians who met him in Mecca had believed. Perhaps he hoped that Jews would also respond positively to his message, discerning in him a 'Clear Sign' from Allah. (Q98) Indeed Muhammad said that what he was teaching was the same as the Jewish religion, including 'performing the prayer' and paying *zakat*. (Q98:5) He even directed his followers to pray facing 'Syria' (al-Sham), which is interpreted to mean towards Jerusalem, copying the Jewish custom. (Q2:144)

When Muhammad arrived in Medina, Islamic tradition records that he implemented a covenant to which the Jews were a party. This covenant recognized the Jewish religion 'the Jews have their religion and the Muslims have theirs' and it commanded loyalty from the Jews to Muhammad.

Opposition in Medina

Muhammad began to present his message to the Jewish residents of Medina, but met with unexpected resistance. Islamic tradition attributes this to envy. Some of Muhammad's revelations included Biblical references, and no doubt the rabbis contested this material, pointing out contradictions with Muhammad's interpretations.

The prophet of Islam found the rabbis' questions troublesome, and at times more of the Quran would be sent down to him, furnishing him with replies. Again and again, when Muhammad would be challenged by a question, he would turn the incident into an opportunity for self-validation, as reflected in the verses of the Quran.

One of Muhammad's simplest strategies was to assert that the Jews were deceivers, quoting passages that suited them, but concealing others which would not have helped their cause. (Q36:76; Q2:77)

Another answer from Allah was that the Jews had deliberately falsified their scriptures. (Q2:75)

The rabbis' conversations with Muhammad were interpreted by Islamic tradition, not as genuine dialogue or reasonable answers to Muhammad's claims, but as *fitna*, an attempt to destroy Islam and the faith of Muslims.

A hostile theology of the rejecters

Muhammad's frustrating conversations with Jews informed his growing hostility to them. Whereas in the past verses had said some Jews were believers, now the Quran declared that the whole Jewish race was cursed and only very few were true believers. (4:46)

The Quran announced that in the past some Jews were transformed into monkeys and pigs for their sins. (Q7:166; Q5:60; Q2:65) Allah also called them prophet-killers. (Q5:70) Allah had renounced his relationship with the covenant-breaking Jews, hardening their hearts, so Muslims can always expect to find them treacherous (except for a few). (Q5:13) Having broken their covenant, the Jews are declared to be 'losers' who have forsaken their true guidance. (Q2:27)

Before he came to Medina, Muhammad's revelations had suggested Judaism was valid. (Q2:62) However this verse was abrogated by Q3:85. In Medina, Muhammad came to the view that he had been sent to correct the errors of the Jews. (Q5:115) He concluded that his coming had abrogated Judaism, that the Islam he brought was the final religion, and the Quran the last revelation. All who rejected this message would be 'losers' (Q3:85). It would no longer be acceptable for Jews – or Christians – to follow their old religion: they had to acknowledge Muhammad, and become Muslims too.

In the verses of the Quran, Muhammad launched a full-frontal theological onslaught upon Judaism. This arose out of a profound offense taken by Muhammad at the Jew's rejection of his message. This was another self-validation for Muhammad, like those he had resorted to with the Meccan idolaters. Then Muhammad went further, and implemented aggressive responses as well.

Rejection turns into violence

In Medina, Muhammad began a campaign to intimidate, and ultimately to eliminate the Jews. Emboldened by victory over the idolaters at Badr, he visited the Qaynuqa' Jewish tribe and threatened them with God's vengeance.

Then, on a pretext, he besieged the Qaynuqa' Jews and expelled them from Medina.

Then Muhammad commenced a series of targeted assassinations of Jews, and issued a command to his followers 'Kill any Jew that falls into your power'. To the Jews he announced *aslim taslam* 'accept Islam and you will be safe'.

A profound shift had taken place in Muhammad's understanding. Non-Muslims had rights to their property and lives only if they had supported and honored Islam and Muslims. Anything else was *fitna*, and a pretext for fighting them.

Muhammad's task of dealing with the Jews was not yet complete. The Banu Nadir were next in line to come under his attention. The whole Nadir tribe was accused of breaking their covenant, so they were attacked, and after an extended siege were likewise driven out of Medina, abandoning their property as booty for the Muslims.

After this, Muhammad besieged the last remaining Jewish tribe, the Qurayza, on the basis of a command from the angel Gabriel. When the Jews surrendered unconditionally, the men were beheaded in the market place of Medina – six to nine hundred by varying accounts – and the Jewish women and children were distributed as booty (i.e. as slaves) among the Muslims.

Muhammad was not quite finished with the Jews of Arabia. After clearing Medina of their presence, he attacked Khaybar. The Khaybar campaign started out with the two-choice scenario: convert or die. However when the Muslims defeated the Jews of Khaybar, a third choice was negotiated: conditional surrender. Thus did the Khaybar Jews become the first *dhimmis*.

This concludes our discussion of Muhammad's dealings with the Jews. It is important to note that the Quran treats Christians and Jews alike as representatives of a single category, the 'People of the Book'. The treatment of Jews in the Quran and the life of Muhammad, as 'People of the Book' became a model for the treatment of Christians down the ages as well.

'We are the victims'

One of the themes of Muhammad's program was an emphasis on the victimhood of Muslims. To sustain the theological position that conquest is liberation, it becomes necessary to seek grounds to find the infidel enemy guilty and deserving of attack. Also, the more extreme the punishment, the more necessary it becomes to insist upon the enemy's guilt. Since, by divine decree Muslims' sufferings were 'worse than slaughter', it became obligatory for Muslims to regard their victimhood as greater than whatever they inflicted upon their enemies. The greater victimhood of Muslims became a doctrinal necessity, a feature of the 'compass of faith' for Muslims.

It is this theological root, grounded in the Quran and the *Sunna* of Muhammad, which explains why, again and again, some Muslims have insisted that their victimhood is greater than that of those they have attacked. This mentality was displayed by Professor Ahmad bin Muhammad, Algerian Professor of Religious Politics, in a debate with Dr Wafa Sultan on Al-Jazeera TV. Infuriated by Dr Sultan's arguments, he began shouting:

> We are the victims! ... There are millions of innocent people among us [Muslims], while the innocent

among you ... number only dozens, hundreds, or thousands, at the most.

This victim mentality continues to plague many Muslim communities to this day, and weakens their capacity to take responsibility for their own actions.

Muhammad the rejecter

This concludes our overview of Muhammad's history of rejection, both received and imposed upon others, and his self-vindicating pursuit of success over his enemies.

As we have seen, the prophet of Islam experienced rejection at many levels: in his family circumstances, from his own community in Mecca, and from the Jews in Medina. In his responses, Muhammad passed through self-rejection, then self-validation, and finally aggression. Muhammad the orphan became the orphan-maker. The self-doubter, who had contemplated suicide because he feared he was being tormented by demons, became the ultimate rejecter, imposing his creed by force of arms to supersede and replace all other faiths.

In Muhammad's emotional worldview, the defeat and degradation of disbelievers would 'heal' his followers' sentiments and quench their rage. This healing 'Islamic peace', won through battle, is described in the Quran. (Q9:14-15)

At first Muhammad and his followers did experience actual persecution at the hands of the Meccan polytheists, but when he assumed power in Medina, Muhammad came to regard even disbelief in his prophethood as persecution, and licensed the use of violence to deal with disbelievers and mockers – whether polytheist, Jew or Christian – so they would be silenced or intimidated into submission. Muhammad instituted an ideological and military program which systematically eliminated all manifestations of rejection expressed towards him and his religious community. He claimed that the success of his program validated and vindicated his prophethood.

The Quran establishes markers along the progress of Muhammad's prophetic career. As such it is revealed as Muhammad's own, intensely personal document, a record of his growing sense of hostility and aggression in the face of rejection. The characteristics which came to be imposed upon non-Muslims, such as silence, guilt and gratitude can be grounded in the evolution of Muhammad's own responses to rejection, and his violent imposition of failure and rejection upon all who refused to confess, 'I believe there is no god but Allah and Muhammad is his prophet.'

CHAPTER 5

Jesus
the Man of Sorrows

A man of sorrows

The life of Jesus, no less than that of Muhammad, is a
story of rejection, the culmination of which is the Cross.
Muhammad responded to persecution with retribution:
Christ's response was entirely different.

Like Muhammad, Jesus' family circumstances were far
from ideal. At birth the stigma of illegitimacy hung
over him (Matthew 1:18-25). He was born in humble
circumstances, in a stable (Luke 2:7). After his birth,
King Herod attempted to kill him. Then he became a
refugee, fleeing to Egypt (Matthew 2:13-18).

Jesus is questioned

When Jesus began his teaching ministry, around the age
of thirty, he experienced a great deal of opposition. As
with Muhammad, Jewish religious leaders would ask

questions of Jesus intended to challenge and undermine his authority:

> ... the Pharisees and the teachers of the law began to oppose him fiercely and to besiege him with questions, waiting to catch him in something he might say. (Luke 11:53-54).

These questions concerned:

- why Jesus was helping people on the Sabbath: this question was to show that he was breaking the law (Mark 3:2; Matthew 12:10);

- what authority he had to do the things he did (Mark 11:28; Matthew 21:23; Luke 20:2);

- whether it is lawful for a man to divorce his wife (Mark 10:2; Matthew 19:3);

- whether it is lawful to pay taxes to Caesar (Mark 12:15; Matthew 22:17; Luke 20:22);

- which is the greatest commandment (Matthew 22:36);

- whose son is the Messiah? (Matthew 22:42);

- Jesus' paternity (John 8:19);

- the resurrection (Matthew 22:23-28; Luke 20:27-33);

- requests to perform signs (Mark 8:11; Matthew 12:38; 16:1).

In addition to the questions, Jesus was accused of:

- being demonized, 'having Satan' and doing miracles by Satan's power (Mark 3:22; Matthew 12:24; John 8:52, 10:20);

- having disciples who did not observe the Sabbath (Matthew 12:2), or the cleanliness rituals (Mark 7:2; Matthew 15:1-2; Luke 11:38); and

- giving invalid testimony (John 8:13).

The rejectors

When we consider Jesus' life and teaching, we find that he experienced rejection from many different individuals and groups:

- King Herod tried to have him killed when he was still an infant (Matthew 2:16).

- People of his own home village at Nazareth took offense at him (Mark 6:3; Matthew 13:53-58), and tried to throw him off a cliff to kill him (Luke 4:28-30).

- His own family members accused him of being out of his mind. (Mark 3:21)

- Many of his followers deserted him (John 6:60).

- A crowd tried to stone him (John 10:31).

- Religious leaders plotted to kill him (John 11:50).

- He was betrayed by Judas, one of his inner circle (Mark 14:43ff, Matthew 26:14-16; Luke 22:1-6; John 18:2-3).

- He was disowned three times by Peter, his chief disciple (Mark 14:66-72; Matthew 26:69-75; Luke 22:54-62; John 18).

- His crucifixion was demanded by a crowd in Jerusalem, a city where he had only a few days earlier welcomed him with shouts of joy as a potential

Messiah (Mark 15:12-15; Luke 23:18-23; John 19:15).

- He was punched, spat upon and mocked by religious leaders (Mark 14:65; Matthew 26:67-8).

- He was mocked and abused by Roman soldiers (Mark 15:16-20; Matthew 27:27-31; Luke 22:63-65, 23:11).

- He was falsely charged before Jewish and Roman tribunals, and sentenced to death (Mark 14:53-65; Matthew 26:57-67; John 18:28ff).

- He was crucified, the most degrading means of execution available to the Romans, which was regarded by Jews a punishment which incurs God's curse (Deuteronomy 21:23).

- Raised between two thieves, Jesus was reviled while enduring his dying agonies on the cross (Mark 15:21-32; Matthew 27:32-44; Luke 23:32-36; John 19:23-30).

Jesus' responses to rejection

When we consider all these rejections, we do not find that Jesus is aggressive or violent. He does not seek revenge.

Sometimes Jesus would simply not respond to charges laid against him, most famously when he was charged before his crucifixion (Matthew 27:14). The early church regarded this as the fulfilment of a Messianic prophecy:

He was oppressed and afflicted, yet he did not open his mouth;
he was led like a lamb to the slaughter, and as a sheep before her shearers is silent, so he did not open his mouth. (Isaiah 53:7)

When he was challenged to prove himself, Jesus would sometimes refuse to do so, preferring to ask a question instead (e.g. Matthew 21:24; 22:15ff). He was not quarrelsome, though many times people tried to pick fights with him:

> He will not quarrel or cry out; no one will hear his voice in the streets. A bruised reed he will not break, and a smoldering wick he will not snuff out, till he leads justice to victory. (Matthew 12:19-20, citing Isaiah 42:1-4)

When people wanted to stone Jesus or kill him, he would just move on to another place, (Luke 4:30) except for the events leading to his crucifixion, when Jesus went deliberately to his death.

The point about these responses is that when Jesus was tempted by experiences of rejection, he overcame the temptation, and did not succumb to the rejection. The letter to the Hebrews summarizes his responses as follows:

> ... we do not have a high priest who is unable to sympathize with our weaknesses, but we have one who has been tempted in every way, just as we are – yet was without sin. (Hebrews 4:15-16)

The picture we have of Jesus in the gospels is of someone who is very secure and at ease with himself, who feels no need to decimate those who come against him. Jesus not only reacted well to rejection, he also taught his disciples a theological framework for responding to rejection, indeed for rejecting rejection. Key elements of this theology are described below.

Jesus' theology of rejection

Embrace rejection

Jesus made clear that it was an essential part of his vocation as God's Messiah to be rejected. God planned to use the rejected one as the keystone for the whole of his building:

> The stone the builders rejected has become the capstone... (Mark 12:11, citing Psalm 118:22-23. Cf. also Matthew 21:42.)

Jesus was identified (e.g. 1 Peter 2:21ff and Acts 8:32-35) as the rejected, suffering servant of Isaiah, through whose sufferings the people will find peace and salvation from their sins:

> He was despised and rejected by men,
> a man of sorrows, and familiar with suffering.
> ...
> But he was pierced for our transgressions,
> he was crushed for our iniquities;
> the punishment that brought us peace was upon him,
> and by his wounds we are healed. (Isaiah 53:3-5)

The cross was the central part of this plan, and Jesus repeatedly referred to the fact that he would be put to death:

> He then began to teach them that the Son of Man must suffer many things and be rejected by the elders, chief priests and teachers of the law, and that he must be killed and after three days rise again. He spoke plainly about this... (Mark 8:31-32; cf also Mark 10:32-34; Matthew 16:21; 20:17-19, 26:2; Luke 18:31; John 12:23)

Reject violence

Jesus explicitly and repeatedly condemned the use of force to achieve his goals, even when his own life was at stake:

> 'Put your sword back into its place,' Jesus said to him, 'for all who draw the sword will die by the sword' (Matthew 26:52).

As Jesus goes to the cross, he renounces the use of force to vindicate his mission, even at the cost of his death:

> Jesus said, 'My kingdom is not of this world. If it were, my servants would have fought to prevent my arrest by the Jews. But now my kingdom is from another place. (John 18:36)

There is a reference to bringing 'a sword' when Jesus was speaking about the future sufferings of the church. He said:

> Do not suppose that I have come to bring peace to the earth. I did not come to bring peace, but a sword. (Matthew 10:34).

Although this is sometimes cited as evidence that Jesus licensed violence, in fact it refers to the divisions which can come within families when Christians are rejected for faith in Christ: the corresponding passage in Luke has the word 'division' instead of 'sword' (Luke 12:51). The sword then is symbolic, standing for that which divides, separating one family member from another. Another possible interpretation, in the broader context of the advice Jesus was giving about future persecutions, is that the 'sword' refers to persecution of Christians. In this case, this is a sword raised against Christians because of their testimony, not by them.

Jesus' rejection of violence was contrary to commonly held expectations about what the Messiah would do when he came to save God's people. The hope had been that this salvation would be military and political as well as spiritual. Jesus rejected the military option. He also made clear that his Kingdom was not political either, when he said it was 'not of this world'. He also taught that people should give Caesar what is Caesar's, and God what is God's (Matthew 22:21). He denied that the Kingdom of God could be located physically, because it was to be found within people (Luke 17:21). When confronted by his disciples, who were arguing about who would get the preferred political office in the Kingdom of God – symbolized by the location of their seating position – Jesus countered that God's Kingdom was not like the political kingdoms they were familiar with, where people lorded it over each other. In order to be 'first', he said, you had to be last (Matthew 20:16, 27) His followers should seek to serve rather than to be served (Mark 10:43; Matthew 10:27).

The early church took Jesus' teachings on violence to heart. For example, among the professions prohibited to the early believers in the first centuries of the church was that of a soldier, and if a Christian did happen to be a soldier, he was prohibited from killing.

Love your enemies

Aggressive reactions to rejection feed upon enmity based upon rejection and condemnation of the other. Jesus taught that retribution was no longer acceptable but only good should be returned for evil received (Matthew 5:38-42); it is wrong to judge others (Matthew 7:1-5); enemies are to be loved, not hated (Matthew 5:43); the meek will inherit the earth (Matthew 5:5); and peacemakers will be called children of God (Matthew 5:9).

These teachings were not mere words, which the disciples listened to and then forgot. Jesus' followers make clear in their letters, preserved in the New Testament, that these principles guided them even in the face of great trials and opposition:

> To this very hour we go hungry and thirsty, we are in rags, we are brutally treated, we are homeless. ... When we are cursed, we bless; when we are persecuted, we endure it; when we are slandered, we answer kindly. (1 Corinthians 4:11-13; cf also 1 Peter 3:10; Titus 3:1-2; Romans 12:14-21)

The apostles held up before believers the example of Jesus himself (1 Peter 2:21-25), and the 'love your enemies' verse of Matthew 5 became the most frequently quoted passage of the Bible in the writings of the early church.

Prepare yourselves for persecution

Persecution, Jesus taught his followers, was inevitable: they would be flogged, hated, betrayed and put to death (Mark 13:9-13; Luke 21:12-19; Matthew 10:17-23).

Jesus warned his disciples, when training them how to take his message to others, that they would experience rejection. In sharp contrast to example and teaching of Muhammad, which encouraged Muslims to respond to suffering with violence and even slaughter, Jesus taught his disciples to simply 'shake the dust off your feet when you leave'. In other words, they should just move on, taking nothing defiling away from their encounter (Mark 6:11; Matthew 10:14). This was not a parting in bitterness, for their peace would 'return' to them (Matthew 10:13).

Jesus himself modelled this, when a Samaritan village refused to welcome him. His disciples had asked him to call down fire from heaven upon them, but Jesus rebuked them and just moved on (Luke 9:54-56).

Jesus taught his disciples that they were to flee to another place when persecuted (Matthew 10:23). They should not worry, because the Holy Spirit will help them know what to say (Mark 10:19-20; Luke 12:11-12, 21:14-15), neither should they be afraid (Mark 10:31; Matthew 10:26).

A distinctive teaching of Jesus was that his followers should rejoice when they are persecuted, because they will be identifying with the prophets:

> Blessed are you when men hate you, when they
> exclude you and insult you and reject your name as
> evil, because of the Son of Man.
> Rejoice in that day and leap for joy, because great is
> your reward in heaven. For that is how their fathers
> treated the prophets.
> (Luke 6:22-23; Matthew 5:11-12).

There is plenty of evidence that this message was wholeheartedly embraced by the early church, as part of their devotion to Christ:

> ... even if you should suffer for what is right, you
> are blessed. (1 Peter 3:14; cf also 1 Corinthians 1:5;
> Philippians 2:17-18; 1 Peter 4:12-14)

Jesus also encouraged his disciples with the hope that, along with persecution, they would receive the gift of eternal life – the best is yet to come – but to receive this promise in the next life they had to remain faithful in this life (Mark 10:29-30, Mark 13:13).

CHAPTER 6

The Cross
our Path to Freedom

Muhammad against the cross

Because we live in a spiritual world, it is noteworthy that
Muhammad hated crosses. A tradition reported by al-
Waqidi said that if ever Muhammad found an object in
his house with the mark of a cross on it, he would destroy
it.[1]

Muhammad's hatred of the cross even extended to
teaching that Jesus would return to the earth as a cross-
destroying prophet of Islam, to eliminate Christianity
from the face of the earth:

> Narrated Abu Huraira:
> Allah's Apostle said, 'By Him in Whose Hands my
> soul is, surely (Jesus,) the son of Mary will soon
> descend amongst you and will judge mankind justly
> (as a Just Ruler); he will break the cross and kill the

---

1 W. Muir, *The life of Muhammad*. Volume 3, p.61, note 47.

pigs and there will be no *jizya* (i.e. taxation taken from non Muslims). ...' (*Sahih al-Bukhari*. The Book of the Stories of the Prophets. 4:60:3448.)

In other words, when Jesus returns, the 'third choice' will disappear, and Christians must convert to Islam or be killed.

Today Muhammad's enmity to the cross is shared by many Muslims:

- Two days before Christmas in 1998, a Catholic church in Faisalabad, Pakistan had its crucifix pulled down by a Muslim leader.[1]

- On March 18, 2004, an Albanian mob attacked and desecrated the church of St Andrew in Podujevo, Kosovo. Photographs distributed to the international media show Muslims, who had climbed up onto the roof, breaking off the prominent metal crosses attached there.[2] There have also been many instances of Muslim mobs smashing crosses in Christian graveyards across Kosovo.[3]

- In April 2007, in the Al-Doura Christian area of Baghdad, Muslim militants instructed Christians to remove visible crosses from atop their churches, and

1 Annual Report on International Religious Freedom for 1999. US State Department. <http://www.thepersecution.org/ussd/us99irf.html>.
2 ERP-KIM Info Service. Newsletter 17/3/2005. <http://www.kosovo.net/news/archive/2005/March_17/1.html>.
3 Jared Israel, 'Eradication of an ancient culture... The destruction of the churches of Kosovo.' <http://emperors-clothes.com/list.htm>.

issued a *fatwa* forbidding Christians from wearing crosses.[1]

- When Hamas took control of Gaza in 2007, some of its militias went on a cross-destroying rampage. The Rosary Sisters convent and school in Gaza was ransacked and looted by masked men and crosses were specifically targeted for destruction. A Christian resident of Gaza also reported having a crucifix ripped from his neck by someone from the Hamas Executive Force, who said 'That is forbidden.'[2]

- On Monday 29 October 2007, in the Malaysian Parliament, Tuan Syed Hood bin Syed Edros complained about the 'display of religious symbols' in front of church schools: 'I, as a responsible person to my religion, race, and country, I state my views that ... these crosses need to be destroyed ...'[3]

- In November 2004, Belmarsh Prison in England was reported to have plans to spend £1.6 million on a mosque. The facility already maintains a multi-denominational chapel, but this has been rejected for use by the Muslim inmates, some of whom had been

1 Extremists threaten church in Baghdad'. Zenit news service. 19 April 2007. <http://www.zenit.org/article-19414?l=english>.
2 Fears in PA: Gaza may turn into Taliban-style Emirate. MEMRI Special Dispatch Series 1633, Palestinian Authority/Jihad & Terrorism Studies Project, June 26, 2007. <http://memri.org/bin/articles.cgi?Page=archives&Area=sd&ID=SP163307>. This is cited from Al-Quds Al-Arabi (London), June 20, 2007.
3 The Hansard record of the Third Meeting of the Fourth Session of Eleventh Parliament (Dewan Rakyat) of Malaysia, on Monday, 29 October 2007, pp.143-44 <http://www.parlimen.gov.my/hindex/pdf/DR-29102007.pdf>.

convicted on terrorism charges, because the chapel contains crosses which have to be covered up when the Muslims say their prayers.[1]

- In another British cross-rejecting incident, a London trainee traffic warden M'hammed Azzaoui complained against wearing the British crown on his uniform, because it has a tiny five millimeter cross upon it. He brought an employment tribunal claim against the Metropolitan Police for 'racial discrimination'. Although the claim was later withdrawn, the police authorities offered a dispensation to those who refuse to wear the insignia of the British crown on religious grounds.

- No less a figure than the former Archbishop of Canterbury George Carey consented to remove his pectoral cross when he had to make a forced stop in Saudi Arabia in 1995. The incident is described by David Skidmore in the Episcopal News Service:

> Carey's flight out of Cairo for Sudan was forced to make an intermediary stop in Saudi Arabia. On the approach to the Red Sea coastal city of Jidda, Saudi Arabia, Carey was told to remove all religious insignia, including his clerical collar and pectoral cross.[2]

Although the cross is rejected by Muslims, for Christians it stands for our freedom.

---

1 Reported by Justin Penrose, writing in the *Sunday Mirror* of November 7. 2004. Daniel Pipes offered a critique of this decision in his 'Londonistan Follies' blog <http://www.danielpipes.org/blog/298>.

2 David Skidmore. 'Heart speaks to heart during Archbishop of Canterbury's visit to Chicago.' <http://www.wfn.org/1996/06/msg00144.html>.

The Cross, rejection and reconciliation

In Christian understanding, the human problem is sin, which alienates humanity from God and from each other. The problem of sin is not just an issue of disobedience. It is a breach in relationship with God. When Adam and Eve disobeyed God, they turned away from him. They chose not to trust God, but to listen to the serpent. They turned their backs on God, rejecting him, and rejecting relationship with him. As a result God rejected them, and excluded them from his presence. They became subject to the curses of the Fall.

In the history of Israel, God had provided a covenant through Moses to re-establish right relationship between God and mankind, but his people disobeyed the commandments and went their own way. In their disobedience, they rejected relationship with God and came under judgement. But God did not reject them utterly: he had a plan for their restoration. He had a plan for their salvation and for the salvation of the world.

Although people rejected God, he did not finally reject them. His heart yearned for the people he had made, and he conceived a plan for their reconciliation. The incarnation and cross of Jesus Christ is the fulfilment of God's plan for the restoration of all humanity in healed relationship with himself.

The key to overcoming the deep issue of human rejection of God and the judgement this brings, is the cross. Jesus' submission to the rejection of the cross provides the key to overcoming rejection itself. The power of rejection is in the reactions which it triggers in the hearts of all humanity. By absorbing the hatred of his attackers, and giving his life as a sacrifice for the sins of the world, Jesus defeated the power of rejection itself, overwhelming it with love. This love which Jesus showed was none other than the love of God for the world which he had made:

> For God so loved the world that he gave his one and only Son, that whoever believes in him shall not perish but have eternal life. (John 3:16)

In his death on the cross, Jesus took upon himself the punishment which was humanity's due for rejecting God. This penalty was death, and Christ bore it so that all people who believe in him will find forgiveness and eternal life. In this way Jesus also overcame the power of rejection, by satisfying its penalty.

The symbolism of sacrifice from the Torah, where it was the shedding of blood which atoned for sin, is applied by Christians to interpret the significance of Jesus' death on the cross. This is expressed in Isaiah's song of the suffering servant:

> ... the punishment that bought us peace was upon him, and by his wounds we are healed. Yet it was the Lord's will to crush him and cause him to suffer, and though the LORD makes his life a guilt offering, he will see the light of life and be satisfied, ... he poured out his life unto death, and was numbered with the transgressors. For he bore the sin of many, and made intercession for the transgressors. (Isaiah 53:5,10,12)

In a powerful passage from his letter to the Romans, Paul explained how the sacrifice of Christ brings an end to rejection by granting us its opposite, reconciliation:

> For if, when we were God's enemies, we were reconciled to him through the death of his Son, how much more, having been reconciled, shall we be saved through his life! Not only is this so, but we also rejoice in God through our Lord Jesus Christ,

through whom we have now received reconciliation. (Romans 5:6-11)

This reconciliation also overcomes all rights of condemnation which might be raised by third parties, including human beings, angels or demons (Romans 8:38):

> Who will bring any charge against those whom God has chosen? It is God who justifies. ... [Nothing] will be able to separate us from the love of God that is in Christ Jesus our Lord. (Romans 8:31-33, 39).

Not only this, but Christians have been entrusted with the ministry of reconciliation, both through extending reconciliation to others, and also through proclaiming the message of the cross and its power to destroy rejection:

> All this is from God, who reconciled us to himself through Christ and gave us the ministry of reconciliation; that God was in Christ, reconciling the world to himself in Christ, not counting men's sins against them. And he has committed to us the message of reconciliation. We are therefore Christ's ambassadors, as though God were making his appeal through us. (2 Corinthians 5:18-20)

The resurrection and vindication

Resurrection

One of the persistent themes of Muhammad's 'revelations' and statements reflect is a desire for vindication. He achieves this for himself by forcing his enemies to submit to his creed, thus placing themselves under his guidance and authority, or else compelling them to accept dhimmitude. Their third alternative was death.

In the Christian understanding of the mission of Christ, there is vindication, but it is not achieved by Christ for himself. The role of the suffering Messiah was to humble himself, embracing rejection. Vindication came through the resurrection and ascension of Christ, through which death and all its power was defeated:

> … he was not abandoned to the grave, nor did his body see decay.
> God has raised this Jesus to life, and we are all witnesses of the fact. Exalted to the right hand of God, he has received from the Father the promised Holy Spirit and has poured out what you now see and hear. … God has made this Jesus… both Lord and Christ. (Acts 2:31-36)

A famous passage from Paul's letter to the Philippians describes how Jesus 'humbled himself', willingly adopting a slave's role. His obedience extended even to death. But God exalted him to a spiritual position of supreme authority. This victory was not due to Christ's own striving but to God's sovereign vindication of his supreme offering of himself upon the cross:

> Your attitude should be the same as that of Christ Jesus: who, being in very nature God,
> did not consider equality with God something to be grasped, but made himself nothing, taking the very nature of a servant, being made in human likeness.
> And being found in appearance as a man,
> He humbled himself and became obedient to death
> – even death on a cross!
> Therefore God exalted him to the highest place
> and gave him the name that is above every name,
> that at the name of Jesus every knee should bow …
> (Philippians 2:4-10)

The discipleship of the cross

For Christians, to follow Christ means identifying with his death and resurrection. Both Jesus and his followers repeatedly refer to the need to 'die' with Christ – that is, to put the old way of living to death – and to be reborn, raised to a new life according to Christ's way of love and reconciliation, not living for ourselves, but for God. Experiences of suffering are regarded as a way of sharing in the sufferings of Christ, which defines the meaning of the trials they were going through, as a pathway through to life, and evidence of impending victory, not defeat. In this it was God who will vindicate the faithful believers, not the brutal powers of this world:

> If anyone would come after me, he must deny himself and take up his cross and follow me. For whoever wants to save his life will lose it, but whoever loses his life for me and for the gospel will save it.' (Mark 8:34-35; cf also 1 John 3:14,16; 2 Corinthians 5:14-15; Hebrews 12:1-2)

Two tales of rejection

It is remarkable that Jesus and Muhammad, the founders of the two largest religions of the world, are both reported to have sustained severe experiences of rejection. These commenced with the circumstances of their birth and infancy, and extended to include dealings with family members and religious authorities. Both were accused of being insane or controlled by evil forces. Both were mocked and reviled. Both suffered betrayal. Both suffered threats to their lives.

However these remarkable similarities are overshadowed by an even more remarkable difference, which had a profound impact on the way in which these two religions were established. Whereas Muhammad's life story demonstrates the full range of negative responses common to humanity, including self-rejection, self-validation and aggression, the life of Jesus went in a completely different direction. He overcame rejection, not by imposing it upon others, but by embracing it, and thereby, according to Christian belief, overcoming its power and healing its pain. If the life of Muhammad contains the keys to understanding the imprisoning spiritual legacy of the *dhimma*, how much more the life of Christ offers keys to freedom and wholeness for Christians who have suffered the effects of dhimmitude.

A Spiritual Worldview

The worldview relied on here has been shaped by the New Testament. Paul in his letter to the Colossians tells them of his prayers for them:

> I pray that you will be grateful to God for letting you have part in what he has promised his people in the kingdom of light. God rescued us from the dark power of Satan and brought us into the kingdom of his dear Son, who forgives our sins and sets us free. (Colossians 1:12-13)

In Paul's view, human beings are by nature under the power of Satan and his demonic powers, but through faith in Christ, they find freedom from the powers of evil. J.H. Houlden, Fellow of Trinity College Oxford, has written an overview of Paul's theological worldview. Paul, he says:

> ... had convictions about man. Not only is man sinfully and wilfully alienated from God ... he is

also under bondage to demonic powers who stalk the universe and who use the Law, not as a means of man's obedience to God, but as an instrument of their tyranny. This alienation of man from God is common to all mankind – it is neither purely Jewish nor purely Gentile. It is the state of man as child of Adam. (*Paul's Letters from Prison*, p.18)

Houlden goes on to explain that, in Paul's worldview, human beings need to be rescued from this bondage: 'As far as the demonic powers are concerned, man's need is simply deliverance from their control.' (p.18). The key to this rescue is what Christ has done through his death and resurrection. This achieved a victory over sin, and the demonic powers of evil which bind humanity.

The apostle John writes in his first letter:

'We know that we are children of God, and that the whole world is under the control of the evil one.' (1 John 5:19)

If the whole world is by nature under the control of the 'dark power of Satan' (Colossians 1:13), as Paul puts it, then a worldview such as Islam, which imposes untold suffering upon communities for centuries must be assessed, not only in political or social terms, but also in spiritual terms, as a specific manifestation of the tyranny of evil in the human sphere.

One must acknowledge that the institutional church is not itself immune from being an agent for evil.

Overcoming the power of evil

For Christians to gain freedom from the pernicious spiritual impact of dhimmitude, it is necessary to confront the power of Satan, who is the ultimate spiritual force behind all rejection in this world.

According to the gospels and the letters of the New Testament, Satan has a genuine but limited power and sovereignty over this world. He is 'the prince of this world' (John 12:31), 'the god of this age' (2 Corinthians 4:4), and 'the ruler of the kingdom of the air' (Ephesians 2:2), whose kingdom is the 'dominion of darkness' (Colossians 1:13). He is the 'spirit who is now at work in those who are disobedient' (Ephesians 2:2).

When Jesus reveals himself to Paul in a vision, and calls him to go to the Gentiles, the apostle is told that he will turn people from 'darkness to light, and from the power of Satan to God' (Acts 26:18), a phrase which indicates that people, before being saved by Christ, are under Satan's power, but through Christ they are redeemed and transferred out from the power of darkness, into the Kingdom of God.

According to the Bible, a spiritual confrontation is going on between God and Satan, which amounts to a cosmic civil rebellion (Mark 1:15; Luke 10:18; Ephesians 6:12). This is a conflict between two kingdoms, in which there is no neutral ground for anyone to hide. Christians find themselves in an extended campaign in which the decisive battle has already been won on the cross, and the final outcome is not in doubt: Christ is and will be victorious.

As agents of Christ, followers of Christ now find themselves engaged in a daily engagement with the powers of this dark age. Christ's death and resurrection provides our sole authority against this darkness, and the basis of our power to stand against it. The contested territory of this warfare consists of people, communities, societies and nations. The institutional church must also be regarded as a battle-ground, and its resources can also be exploited for evil purposes.

Our focus here however is with Islam, and in this case a key point of spiritual engagement must be to challenge the spiritual and territorial claims of the *dhimma* and *shahada* pacts, which on the one hand have enslaved Muslims in a false sense of superiority and schooled them to become oppressors of others, and on the other hand have enslaved Christians and other non-Muslims in humiliation, false gratitude and silence, placing them under a curse of death (Ephesians 6:11-17).

Paul describes the certainty of victory when he writes that the powers of this dark age have been disarmed, disgraced and defeated, through the cross and the forgiveness of sins which it effects:

> When you were dead in your sins and in the uncircumcision of your sinful nature, God made you alive with Christ. He forgave us all our sins, having cancelled the written code, with its regulations, that was against us and that stood opposed to us; he took it away, nailing it to the cross. And having disarmed the powers and authorities, he made a public spectacle of them, triumphing over them by the cross. (Colossians 2:13-15).

The *dhimma* and *shahada* are instances of such a 'written code' which stands opposed to our common humanity. The spiritual power of all that these codes represent can be dealt with by applying the power of the cross to all their bitter and rejecting claims, in effect by 'nailing' the *dhimma* pact and the *shahada* to the cross. This includes a public demonstration of their false claims, as I have sought to do in *The Third Choice*.

A key aspect of the *dhimma's* power is the silence it imposes upon non-Muslims, and in exposing its character, we nail it to the cross and declare it to be disarmed and toothless. By engaging spiritually in this way, Christians are able to reject and stand against the spiritual principles and powers which underpin the *dhimma* pact.

Legal rights

One of the key steps to finding spiritual freedom consists of renouncing all spiritual claims which Satan might make against us. Spiritual commitments, even those made by past generations, can impact profoundly upon our ability to live free in Christ. Covenants made and traumas experienced can serve as grounds which Satan uses to perpetuate his oppression of us.

In order to motivate the need for renunciation, it is useful to discuss Satan's legal rights to oppress peoples, including the concepts of doorways and footholds. A doorway is an entry point which someone may grant to Satan through disobedience, and which Satan then exploits to attack and oppress the person. A foothold is internal surrendered ground within the human soul, which a person has given over to Satan. Paul refers to the possibility that a Christian could give opportunity to the devil by harbouring anger:

> Do not let the sun go down while you are still angry, and do not give the devil a foothold. (Ephesians 4:26-27)

The Greek word translated here as 'foothold' is *topos* 'a place'. Topos has the core meaning of an inhabited or occupied place, and the expression 'give a place' conveys the implication of 'give opportunity'. Paul is saying that if someone hangs onto anger, rather than confessing and renouncing it as sin, they have surrendered spiritual ground to be occupied and manipulated for evil purposes.

In John 14:30, Jesus uses the language of legal rights when he states that Satan has no hold on him:

> I will not speak with you much longer, for the prince of this world is coming. He has no hold on me, but the world must learn that I love the Father and that I do exactly what my Father has commanded me. (John 14:30-31)

Archbishop J.H. Bernard writes in his commentary on this passage that Jesus is saying 'Satan ... has no point in my personality on which he can fasten'. (*A Critical and Exegetical Commentary on the Gospel According to John*, vol. 2, p. 556). The idiom here is in fact a legal one, as is explained by Carson:

> He has no hold on me is an idiomatic rendering of 'he has nothing in me', recalling a Hebrew idiom frequently used in legal contexts, 'he has no claim on me', 'he has nothing over me'. ... The devil could have a hold on Jesus only if there were a justifiable charge against Jesus. (*The Gospel According to John*, pp.508-9.)

It is Jesus' lack of sin – 'I do exactly what my Father has commanded me' – which he gives as the reason why there is nothing in him which allows Satan to claim any legal rights. This is of profound importance for our understanding of the cross, because Jesus' death is something over which Satan could claim no rights in terms of it being a lawful penalty. The death of the Lord's Messiah was an innocent sacrifice on behalf of others, not

Liberty to the Captives

a just penalty enacted against Jesus by Satan. If Christ had surrendered ground to Satan, his death would have been a just punishment for sin: instead it was an effective offering on behalf of the sins of the whole world.

Closing off entry points

When claiming spiritual freedom, it is sensible and necessary to systematically attend to, identify, and close all doorways, and remove the footholds in one's life. Closing doorways includes repentance by a person for any words or deeds by which they may have given permission for Satan to claim rights over their life. This entails a 'truth encounter' whereby any evil lies or deceptions to which a person has submitted are confessed and renounced. The power of the cross is the key to this process. By appealing to Christ as Saviour, an individual receives God's forgiveness, and in being buried with Christ, becomes identified with him, and is one against whom Satan can make no lawful charge, and over whom he no longer has any hold.

How does this work in practice? If someone is struggling with a habit of persistent lying, then that person needs to be able to recognize that lying is wrong in God's sight, confess this, repent of lying and be assured of forgiveness through the work of Christ. When this is done, lying itself can be rejected and renounced. If, on the other hand, the person likes lying, finds it useful, and has no intention of giving it up, any bid for freedom from lying is likely to be futile.

A foothold can also consist of a wound in the soul. If someone has been plagued by fears, which had initially attacked them because of a traumatic and terrifying event such as an assault, it may prove necessary to pray for the healing of the trauma, after which the person can be led to renounce the fear and affirm trust in God. The person should also be led through a process of forgiving whoever had inflicted the trauma on them. After this has happened, fear can be much more successfully resisted.

Once when I was teaching on dhimmitude, I was approached by a South African woman who had a traumatic experience involving people from a Muslim background a decade earlier. At the request of a local seminary, her family had offered hospitality to two men. This was the start of an extremely trying and damaging time. Her house guests were aggressive and mocked her and her family continually. They would push her against the walls, call her a 'pig', curse her and even spit on her as they walked past. She even found small pieces of paper lodged in different places all around her home with curses written on them in Arabic. The family asked for help from their church, but no-one would believe them. In the end they were only able to get rid of these 'guests' by renting alternative accommodation for them. The woman writes 'At that time, we were financially, spiritually, emotionally and physically drained and rock bottom. I did not believe in myself any more, I felt I was good for nothing, because they treated me like dirt.' After hearing the presentation on dhimmitude, she confronted the fears and self-doubt which had plagued her, and we prayed together for healing of the traumatic experiences, renouncing intimidation. She was wonderfully healed and said 'I praise the Lord for this heavenly appointment ... . I feel relieved and worthy to serve the Lord as a woman. Praise the Lord!' Later she wrote to me:

> We still serve the Lord, we love Him more than before, we learnt so much of the Muslim culture and

beliefs and we became stronger through all of this and we can say that we love the Muslims with the love of the Lord and will never stop showing them through our lives, how much Jesus loves each one of them.

There is only one pathway to complete freedom from spiritual oppression, and that is the cross of Christ. Certainly, many are the doorways and footholds which Satan uses, but what is important for us here is that the *dhimma* and the *shahada* are two such ways. This leads us to the next important point: intergenerational pathways of oppression.

Intergenerational pathways

It is hardly controversial that certain family lineages demonstrate that damage can be perpetuated from generation to generation. Most would accept the possibility that genetic or social conditions could influence particular families for good or for ill. But do families also pass on a spiritual inheritance? It seems that they can, and some entry points for oppression can be intergenerational. Spiritual oppression can affect multiple generations, as one generation binds the next, inviting the influence of evil in their family.

Some Christians find the concept of intergenerational spiritual bondage to be unacceptable, or even irrational. They may point instead to the influence of parental behaviors on children. For example, if a father is a liar, then his children could copy him, and learn to be liars too. Or if a mother curses her child, the child could have a poor self-image as a result. No doubt copied behavior, and the intergenerational damage caused by parental abuse, are significant factors which help to replicate the effects of sin from one generation to the next, but such considerations cannot fully explain the total range of spiritual oppression which people coming from spiritually dark family backgrounds experience. In my view the evidence for inter-generational spiritual bondage is absolutely clear.

The whole worldview of the Bible in relation to covenants, curses and blessings, is also fully consistent with this view. The Torah describes how God covenanted with the nation of Israel, dealing with them as an inter-generational community and binding them into a system of blessings and curses applying to them and their descendants, the blessings to the thousandth generation, and the curses to the third or fourth generation (Exodus 20:5; 34:7). Furthermore, in order for succeeding generations to be free of the effects of their ancestors' sins, they needed to 'confess their sins and the sins of their fathers' (Leviticus 26: 40). Then, God says, he will 'remember the covenant with their ancestors' and heal them and their land (Leviticus 26: 45).

Since God has dealt with people intergenerationally in this way, why then would not Satan claim intergenerational rights against humankind? Indeed Satan 'the accuser', who 'accuses them before our God day and night' (Revelation 12:10), can and does claim against people the intergenerational rights given to him by virtue of their broken covenants with God. For example Adam and Eve's sin unleashed intergenerational curses against their descendants, including pain in childbirth (Genesis 3:16), dominance of men over women (Genesis 3:16), hard labour to eke out a living (Genesis 3:17-18) and ultimately death and decay (Genesis 3:19).

The scriptures do herald a change in these affairs, that God will no longer hold people to account for their parents' sins, but each person will be responsible for their own sins:

> Yet you ask, 'Why does the son not share the guilt of his father?' Since the son has done what is just and right and has been careful to keep all my decrees, he will surely live. The soul who sins is the one who will die. The son will not share the guilt of the father, nor will the father share the guilt of the son. The righteousness of the righteous man will be credited to him, and the wickedness of the wicked will be charged against him. (Ezekiel 18:19-20)

This passage is to be read as a prophecy for the Messianic Age. It is not a fundamental change in the way 'this dark world' works under Satan's rule, but a promise about the in-breaking of the Kingdom of the Son of God. It is a promise, not only that under the new covenant God will deal with each person according to their own sins, but also that the power of Satan to bind people through their parents' and ancestors' sins will be broken by the power of the death and resurrection of Jesus Christ. The covenant of the old law, the 'law of sin and death' did speak of sins being passed on from one generation to another, but in Christ this old law, by which Satan claimed rights to bind people to their parents' sins, is to be set aside and rendered null and void.

It is essential to understand that the *dhimma* pact is both intergenerational and communal. It is a covenant made by a non-Muslim community which is intended to apply forever, until the end of time. Men enter into this covenant and ratify it by paying *jizya* on behalf of their wives, children and descendants. In Islamic law, once a territory and its people come under Islamic control, they remain forever the property of the Umma.

In practice what this means is that people whose ancestors were subjected to the *dhimma* can suffer under the spiritual bondage of their forebears 'to the third and fourth generation' (Exodus 20:5; 34:7). This accounts in part for the fear and psychological servitude to Islam which can be observed in the *dhimmi* syndrome, even one or two generations removed from life under the *dhimma*.

The *shahada* pact is also intergenerational in its claims, in that Islamic law decrees that the child of a Muslim is also a Muslim.

Testimonies of Renouncing the *shahada*

"Renounce Islam!"

The testimony of a former Muslim who embraced the Christian faith:

'I was raised in a Muslim family in the West. We did attend mosque and learned to say our prayers in Arabic. Beyond that, I was not too religious growing up. Things changed when I went through a period of searching as I went off to university. At the end of this period, I discovered who Jesus Christ really was, and He saved my soul.

I got involved with a student Christian group at the campus. Every week, a different student took turns sharing a message from the Bible. I had been a Christian less than a year, but they asked me if I might share a message nevertheless. The evening I was supposed to share, I stepped into one of the campus libraries for some prayer. My message was, "Jesus Died For Me; Would I Die for Jesus?"

As I began to pray, something very strange happened. I felt a tightening in my throat as if I was being strangled or suffocated. Panic came upon me as this sensation continued and intensified. Then I felt a voice telling me, "Renounce Islam! Renounce Islam!" I believed it was the Lord. At the same time, my mind rationalized: "Lord, I haven't really been 'into' Islam or practicing at all lately."

However, the sense of suffocation continued, so I said, "I renounce Islam." All of this was happening somewhat quietly, since it was a library. Immediately, the sense of pressure around my throat was released. A feeling of great relief came over me! I went back to prayer and preparation for the meeting. At the meeting the Lord really showed up in power and I remember students on their knees and faces crying out to the Lord and offering themselves to Him.'

Discipling new believers

A ministry in North America runs regular intensive training for people of a Muslim background who have accepted Christ as their Lord and saviour. The course coordinators found that the participants experienced many persistent discipleship difficulties. They became aware of the prayers in this book for renouncing the *shahada* and decided to invite all course participants to use these prayers to renounce Islam together. The participants' response was one of great relief and joy. They asked 'Why didn't anyone explain that we needed to renounce Islam. We should have done this long ago!'

The renunciation of Islam is now an essential part of the training course.

Testimonies of Renouncing the *dhimma*

Trans-generational fears

One woman who I prayed with suffered from fear in various areas of her life. Her ancestors had lived as dhimmis in Damascus, Syria a hundred years earlier, where a famous genocide of Christians took place in 1860. When we stepped through prayers renouncing the *dhimma* pact, the power of fear was broken, and she found significant relief from fear in her daily life.

Freedom from the legacy of genocide

A man from an Armenian background had ancestors who had survived the genocide by adopting Greek names, and escaping through Smyrna to Egypt. The best part of a century later, this son of refugees suffered from oppressive fears on a daily basis. He could not leave home without experiencing great anxiety about whether he had locked all the doors and windows. However when he renounced intergenerational fear associated with the trauma of past genocides, and we prayed together for his release, he expressed significant spiritual healing and freedom.

From fear to boldness: evangelism training

A group of Arab speaking Christians used the prayers provided here as part of their preparations for an outreach to Muslims who were visiting a European country as tourists. Although the team were in a free country, yet they confessed to feeling fearful about sharing their faith.

This discussion opened their hearts to the need for healing from fear. One leader explained: 'The fear lives inside you because of the covenant made on your behalf.' After discussing the explanations of the *dhimma* pact, people prayed prayers for freedom together, and renounced the *dhimma* pact. On the last day of the program, there was an evaluation:

> 'The results were amazing. Without any exception all those who attended expressed powerfully that this was an essential ministry training topic and a cause for deep blessings and true freedom, especially that everyone had the opportunity to renounce the *dhimma* covenant and declare their covenant with Jesus through his blood. Praise God there is freedom from this pact in the blood of Jesus, through prayer.'

A Coptic Christian tells how she gained power to evangelize Muslims

'I studied the Sharia as a major subject for four years as a part of my law degree in an Islamic country. I studied in detail the degradation of Christians under Sharia Law, including the *dhimma* regulations, but something was blocking my understanding of the personal impact of such teachings upon my character. I was a committed Christian and loved the Lord Jesus Christ, but I failed time after time to declare him as my Lord in front of my Muslim friends, lest I hurt their feelings.

When I attended a presentation on dhimmitude I felt that my spiritual condition was being brought into the light, and the deep frustrations in my soul were being exposed. I was remembering many situations when I had happily accepted and even defended the superiority of Muslims in their conquered territory, the land of my ancestors. I became convicted that for many years I had accepted and lived out the degradation of being a *dhimmi*. I sought prayer, and instantly experienced great freedom in Christ.

That same night I went back home and called a close Muslim friend. I told her that Jesus Christ loves her and that he died on the cross for her. Since then my ministry to Muslims has become very effective and I have seen many of them declaring Christ as their Lord and Saviour.'

Blood pacts and their renunciation

Another important conceptual key is that, as we have seen, the *dhimma* is a 'blood pact'. In the Hebrew scriptures, a standard way of binding oneself in a covenant was by blood-sacrifice. When God makes his famous covenant with Abraham in Genesis 15, it is enacted through a sacrifice. Abraham provides the animal, slaughters it and lays the parts of the animal on the ground. Then a smoking flame – representing the presence and participation of God – passes along between the parts of the animal. Such rituals invoke a curse, which may or may not be stated explicitly, to the effect of 'may I become like this animal if I break this covenant', i.e. be killed and cut in pieces.

This is reflected in the warning given by God through the prophet Jeremiah that:

> **The men who have violated my covenant and have not fulfilled the terms of the covenant they made before me, I will treat like the calf they cut in two and then walked between its pieces.** The leaders of Judah and Jerusalem, the court officials, the priests and all the people of the land who walked between

91

the pieces of the calf, I will hand over to their enemies who seek their lives. (Jeremiah 34:18-20)

Occult initiation rituals, such as are practiced in witchcraft, can involve binding a person in a pact through the use of blood sacrifice. For other occult groups, death is invoked symbolically, for example by curses of self-destruction, by wearing a symbol of death such as a noose around the neck, or by a ritualized enactment of death, such as being placed in a coffin or a symbolic stabbing to the heart. The traditional Islamic *jizya* payment ceremony, with its ritual 'decapitation' blow to the neck of a non-Muslim is a symbolic blood ritual. This ritual invokes a curse of death, which the *dhimma* brings upon himself and his community, in essence stating spiritually: 'May we be decapitated if I ever break any of the conditions of this pact.'

Blood-pacts invoked through explicit or implied curses are spiritually dangerous because they set up doorways for spiritual oppression. First they bind the person to the conditions of the pact, and then they establish psycho-spiritual permissions for the person to be oppressed, in accordance with the curses invoked by the pact.

The manifestations of these permissions can be quite surprising. One woman from a *dhimmi* background had been suffering from nightmares in which deceased relatives were beckoning to her to come to the land of the dead. She had also been plagued with completely illogical suicidal thoughts, for which there was no apparent explanation. As we talked and prayed, it emerged that other members of her family, in previous generations, had also had inexplicable nightmares about death which troubled them greatly. I discerned that because her ancestors had lived under the *dhimma* for generations, the fear of death was oppressing her. We prayed against this, rebuking the power of death, and cancelling the specific curse of death due to her ancestors' participation in the annual *jizya* payment ritual. After these prayers the woman experienced great relief from the nightmares and thoughts of death.

Authority to loose

When pursuing freedom, it is necessary to take specific actions which counteract and renounce specific ungodly commitments. The Old Testament, where idols and their high places are commanded to be completely destroyed, provides a model of how to ransack the idols' spiritual territory (Deuteronomy 12:1-3): the high places, ritual sites, ritual objects, and altars must be completely destroyed, together with the idols themselves.

Where pacts have been entered into, they need to be revoked one by one, together with each of their conditions and consequences. This needs to be specific. Just as it is usually helpful to name one's sins specifically in confession, so also in claiming spiritual freedom: this shines the light of God's truth into each and every area which needs forgiveness.

The same principle of specificity applies to ungodly covenants. For example, a person who has bound themselves to a vow of silence through a blood sacrifice needs to repent of and renounce participation in this ritual and specifically annul their vow made through it. Likewise someone struggling from unforgiveness, who has uttered over their life such words as 'I will never forgive so-and-so as long as I live', must repent of this vow, renounce the commitment which it represents, and ask for God's forgiveness for uttering it. A victim of sexual abuse, who has agreed to remain silent on pain of death, will need to renounce their vow of silence, e.g. 'I renounce my silence about what has been done to me, and claim the right to speak out.' For someone seeking freedom from the spiritual effects of dhimmitude, it is necessary to renounce the *jizya* payment, and the symbolic ritual blow on the neck which accompanied it.

Jesus himself instructed the disciples that they had power to 'bind' and to 'loose' affairs in the heavens and upon the earth, which is to say, in the spiritual realm and also in the physical domain.

> I tell you the truth, whatever you bind on earth will be (or: has been) bound in heaven, and whatever you loose on earth will be (or: has been) loosed in heaven. (Matthew 18:18, cf. also 16:19)

It is a wonderful comfort that Christians do have the authority to break ungodly pacts and vows, because the covenant in the blood of Christ annuls the power of every pact made for evil purposes. This is a promise expressed in a Messianic passage in Zechariah:

> As for you, because of the blood of my covenant with you, I will free your prisoners from the waterless pit. (Zechariah 9:11)

Through the cross, God informs us, victory has been achieved over the powers and principalities of this dark age (Colossians 2:13-15). This triumph plunders the evil powers and takes away their rights to rule, including those given to them through covenants which people have entered into, willingly or unwillingly, knowingly or inadvertently.

CHAPTER 7

How to Renounce the *Dhimma*

Christian prayers are provided in this chapter which offer a way to find release from the oppressive effects of dhimmitude.

Muhammad's life was shaped by deep experiences of rejection, leading to a wounded spirit, a spirit of offense, a victim mentality, a spirit of violence and a will to dominate others. His calls for *jihad* 'striving' were driven by this oppressed spiritual condition, which sought release through the degradation of others.

In contrast, Christ was rejected, but refused to take offense, refused to take up violence, refused to dominate others, refused to adopt a wounded spirit. His cross and resurrection defeated rejection and the powers of darkness.

Why prayer?

You may wish to pray these prayers for several different reasons:

- You or your ancestors have lived as non-Muslims under Islamic rule, and accepted a *dhimma* pact, or have lived under conditions influenced by the principles of *jihad* and dhimmitude. You may, for example, be afraid of a *jihadi* terrorist attack.

- Your personal or family history may have been deeply impacted by traumatic events, such as experiences of violence associated with *jihad* or other abuses which can occur under *dhimma* conditions. You may not even have heard of such events, but may suspect that they are a part of your family history.

- You or your ancestors have been threatened by the Islamic *jihad*, and although there is no history of actually living under Islam, you wish to be free of the fear and intimidation.

- You or your ancestors have lived as Muslims and you wish to renounce being a party to the *dhimma* pact and all its implications.

These prayers are designed to cancel the *dhimma* pact, together with all its implications, so that it will have no authority over your life. They are designed to resist and break all curses made against you or your ancestors because of being a *dhimmi* living in an Islamic state.

You may also be saying these prayers with a sense of sorrow for lack of knowledge in the past, and wish to stand in the truth of God's word. These prayers are designed to counter all the negative spiritual influences of dhimmitude, such as:

- Hurt
- Fear
- Intimidation
- Shame
- Feelings of Guilt
- Feelings of inferiority
- Self-hatred and self-rejection
- Hatred of others
- Depression
- Deception
- Humiliation
- Withdrawal and Isolation
- Silence

Verses of scripture

The first step in preparing yourself for these prayers is to read verses of scripture. This is to affirm important truths, which underpin the prayers. It is suggested that you do this together with another person who can be your witness to saying these prayers.

God's love overcomes rejection

> And so we know and rely on the love God has for us. God is love. Whoever lives in love lives in God, and God in him. (1 John 4:16)

> [Jesus said:] For God so loved the world that he gave his one and only Son, that whoever believes in him shall not perish but have eternal life. (John 3:16)

Our inheritance is not intimidation: it is in God

> For God did not give us a spirit of fear, but a spirit of power, of love and of self-control. (2 Timothy 1:7)

> For you did not receive a spirit that makes you a slave again to fear, but you received the Spirit of sonship. And by him we cry, 'Abba Father'. The Spirit himself testifies with our spirit that we are God's children, heirs of God and co-heirs with Christ, if indeed we share in his sufferings in order that we also share in his glory. (Romans 8:15-16)

We are called to live in freedom

> [Jesus said:] Then you will know the truth, and the truth will set you free. (John 8:32)

> It is for freedom Christ has set us free. Stand firm, then, and do not let yourselves be burdened again by a yoke of slavery. (Galatians 5:1)

Our bodies belong to God and not to oppression: our blood price has already been paid

> Do you not know that your body is a temple of the Holy Spirit, who is in you, whom you have received from God? You are not your own; you were bought at a price. Therefore honor God with your body. (1 Corinthians 6:19-20)

> They will overcome by the blood of the Lamb ... (Revelation 12:11)

Men and women are equal before God, and one group is not superior over another

> ... there is neither Jew nor Greek, slave nor free, male nor female, for you are all one in Christ Jesus. (Galatians 3:28)

Our distinctive marks are not humiliation or inferiority, but Christ's victory, unity in Christ's love, and the cross

> But thanks be to God, who always leads us in triumphal procession in Christ and through us spreads everywhere the fragrance of the knowledge of him. For we are to God the aroma of Christ among those who are being saved and those who are perishing. (2 Corinthians 2:14)

> May they be brought to complete unity to let the world know that you sent me and have loved them even as you have loved me. (John 17:23)

> [Jesus said:] If anyone would come after me, he must deny himself and take up his cross daily and follow me. (Luke 9:13)

We have the power of the Holy Spirit to reveal the truth

> [Jesus said:] Unless I go away, the Counsellor will not come to you; but if I go, I will send him to you. When he comes, he will convict the world of guilt in regard to sin and righteousness and judgment... (John 16:7-8)

> [Jesus said:] But when he, the Spirit of truth, comes, he will guide you into all truth. (John 16:13)

We have authority in Christ to overcome shame

> Let us fix our eyes on Jesus, the author and perfecter of our faith, who for the joy set before him endured the cross, scorning its shame, and sat down at the right hand of the throne of God. (Hebrews 12:2)

We have the right and the responsibility to educate ourselves and our children about spiritual matters

Only be careful, and watch yourselves closely so that you do not forget the things your eyes have seen or let them slip from your heart as long as you live. Teach them to your children and to their children after them. (Deuteronomy 4:9)

We have authority in Christ to speak the truth in love, with boldness

Death and life are in the power of the tongue, and those who love it will eat its fruit. (Proverbs 18:21)

Now Lord consider their threats and enable your servants to speak your word with great boldness. (Acts 4:29)

Love does not delight in evil but rejoices with the truth. (1 Corinthians 13:6)

If anyone acknowledges that Jesus is the Son of God, God lives in him and he in God. (1 John 4:15)

So do not throw away your confidence; it will be richly rewarded. (Hebrews 10:35)

We can have confidence in the word of truth

God's testimony is greater, because it is the testimony about his Son. (1 John 5:9)

They overcame ... by the word of their testimony. (Revelation 12:11)

We are not defenceless or weaponless, but are spiritually armed in Christ

Finally be strong in the Lord and in his mighty power. Put on the full armor of God, so that you can take your stand against the devil's schemes. (Ephesians 6:10)

For though we live in the world, we do not wage war as the world does. The weapons we fight with are not the weapons of the world. On the contrary, they have divine power to demolish strongholds. We demolish arguments and every pretension that sets itself up against the knowledge of God, and we take captive every thought to make it obedient to Christ. (2 Corinthians 10:3-4)

We can consider it a joy to suffer in Christ's name

Consider it pure joy, my brothers, whenever you face trials of many kinds … (James 1:2; cf Philippians 1:29)

The cross destroys Satan's power and draws us to freedom in Christ

[Jesus said:] Now the prince of this world will be driven out, but I, when I am lifted up from the earth, will draw all people to myself. (John 12:30)

The cross cancels the *dhimma* pact and destroys all its power

When you were dead in your sins and in the uncircumcision of your sinful nature, God made you alive with Christ. He forgave us all our sins, having cancelled the written code, with its regulations, that was against us and that stood opposed to us; he took it away, nailing it to the cross. And having disarmed the powers and authorities, he made a public spectacle of them, triumphing over them by the cross. (Colossians 2:13)

Understand as you pray that your prayers and declarations are powerful and effective. Agree with God that he wills to bring you into complete freedom. Agree in your spirit to accept the truth that Christ has accepted you, and wants to set you free from all the snares of the evil one. Resolve to confront and reject the lie which the *dhimma* pact imposes upon non-Muslims.

Prayers and Declarations

Prayers of confession

Loving God, I confess that I have sinned and turned away from you. I repent and turn towards Christ as my Saviour and Lord. Please forgive me specifically for any times when I have intimidated others, and sought to impose inferiority, or humiliation on others. Forgive me for my pride. Forgive me for any times where I have abused or dominated others. I renounce all these things in Jesus Name.

God and Father of our Lord Jesus Christ, I praise you for the gift of forgiveness won by Christ on the cross. I acknowledge that you have accepted me. I thank you that through the cross we are reconciled to you and to each other. I declare today that I am your child (son/daughter) and an inheritor of the Kingdom of God.

Declarations and Renunciations

Father, I agree with you that I am not subject to fear, but am a child of your love. I reject and renounce the demands of Islam as taught by Muhammad. I renounce all forms of submission to 'Allah of the Quran', and declare that I worship the God of our Lord Jesus Christ alone.

*We repent of the sins of our ancestors in submitting to the **dhimma** pact and its principles, and ask your forgiveness for their sins.*

I renounce and revoke all pacts of surrender made by myself, or my ancestors to the community and principles of Islam.

*I completely reject the **dhimma** and every one of its conditions. I renounce the blow on the neck in the **jizya** payment ritual, together with all that it represents. I specifically renounce the curse of decapitation and death symbolized by this ritual.*

*I declare that the **dhimma** pact is nailed to the cross of Christ. The dhimma has been made a public spectacle, and has no power or rights over me. I declare that the spiritual principles of the dhimma pact are exposed, disarmed, defeated and disgraced through the cross of Christ.*

I renounce false feelings of gratitude to Islam.

I renounce false feelings of guilt.

I renounce deception and lies.

I renounce all agreements to keep silent about my faith in Christ.

*I renounce all agreements to keep silent about the **dhimma** or Islam.*

I will speak and I will not be silent.

I declare that 'The truth shall set me free' (John 8:32) and I choose to live as a free person in Christ Jesus.

I renounce and cancel all curses spoken against me and my family in the name of Islam. I renounce and cancel all curses spoken against my ancestors.

I specifically renounce and break the curse of death. Death, you have no power over me!

I declare that these curses have no power over me.

I claim the blessings of Christ as my spiritual inheritance.

I renounce intimidation. I choose to be bold in Christ Jesus.

I renounce manipulation and control.

I renounce abuse and violence.

I renounce fear. I renounce the fear of being rejected. I renounce the fear of losing my property and possessions. I renounce the fear of poverty. I renounce the fear of being enslaved. I renounce the fear of rape. I renounce the fear of being isolated. I renounce the fear of losing my family. I renounce the fear of being killed and the fear of death.

I renounce the fear of Islam. I renounce the fear of Muslims.

I renounce the fear of being involved in public or political activity.

I declare that Jesus Christ is Lord of all.

I submit to Jesus as Lord of every area of my life. Jesus Christ is Lord of my home. Jesus Christ is Lord of my city. Jesus Christ is Lord of my nation. Jesus Christ is Lord of all peoples in this land. I submit to Jesus Christ as my Lord.

I renounce humiliation. I declare that Christ has accepted me. I serve him and him alone.

I renounce shame. I declare that through the cross I am cleansed from all sin. Shame has no rights over me and I will reign with Christ in glory.

Lord, forgive me and my ancestors for all hatred towards Muslims. I renounce hatred towards Muslims and all others, and declare the love of Christ for Muslims and all other people on this earth.

I repent of the sins of the church and of wrongful submission of church leaders.

I renounce alienation. I declare that I am forgiven and accepted by God through Christ. I am reconciled to God. No power in heaven or on earth can make any charge against me before the throne of God.

I declare my praise and thanks to God our Father, to Christ who is my only Saviour, and to the Holy Spirit who alone gives me life.

I commit myself to be a living witness to Jesus Christ as Lord. I am not ashamed of his cross. I am not ashamed of his resurrection.

I declare I am a child of the living God, the God of Abraham, Isaac and Jacob.

I declare the victory of God and of his Messiah. I declare that every knee will bow and every tongue confess that Jesus Christ is Lord to the glory of God the Father.

I declare forgiveness towards Muslims for participating in the system of dhimmitude.

Father God, please free me from the dhimma, the spirit of dhimmitude, and every ungodly principle attached to the dhimma pact.

I ask now that you fill me with your Holy Spirit, and pour upon me all the blessings of the Kingdom of Jesus Christ. Grant me grace to understand the truth of your Word clearly and apply it in every area of my life. Grant to me words of hope and life, as you promised you would, and bless my lips so I can speak them to others with authority and power in Jesus' name. Give me the boldness to be a faithful witness to Christ. Grant me a deep love for Muslim people and a passion to share the love of Christ with them.

I declare and ask these things in the Name of Jesus Christ my Lord and Savior. Amen.

CHAPTER 8

How to Renounce the *Shahada*

The prayers in this chapter are in four parts. They cover:

- making a commitment to follow Jesus Christ,
- the *shahada* and Muhammad's example,
- deception, and
- superiority.

Prayer of Commitment to Follow Jesus Christ

I believe in one God, the creator, almighty Father.

I renounce all other so-called 'gods'.

I acknowledge that I have sinned against God and against other people. In this I have disobeyed God and rebelled against him and his laws.

I cannot rescue myself from my sins.

I believe Jesus is the Christ, the risen Son of God. He died on the cross in my place and took upon himself the judgment for my sins. He was raised from the dead for me.

I turn away from my sins.

I ask for Christ's gift of forgiveness, won on the cross.

I receive this gift of forgiveness now.

I choose to accept God as my Father, and desire to become his.

I seek the gift of eternal life.

I hand over the rights to my life to Christ and invite him to rule as Lord of my life from this day on.

I renounce all other spiritual allegiances. I specifically renounce the shahada and all its claims over me.

I reject Satan and all evil. I break all ungodly agreements I have made with evil spirits or principles of evil.

I renounce all ungodly ties to others who have exercised an ungodly authority over me.

I renounce all ungodly covenants made by my ancestors on my behalf, which have impacted upon me in any way.

I renounce all psychic or spiritual abilities that do not come from God through Jesus Christ.

I ask for the gift of the promised Holy Spirit.

Father God, please free and transform me so I can bring glory to you and you alone.

Release in me the fruit of the Holy Spirit so I can honour you and love others.

I declare before human witnesses and before all spiritual authorities that I consecrate and bind myself to God through Jesus Christ.

I declare that I am a citizen of Heaven. God is my protector. With the help of the Holy Spirit I choose to submit to and follow Jesus Christ and him alone as Lord all my days.

Freedom from the *shahada* and Muhammad's Example

When Muslims recite the *shahada*, saying that Muhammad is Allah's Messenger, they endorse the Quran as the word of Allah. This also means they accept what the Quran says about Muhammad, including the obligation to follow his example, the threats and curses which fall upon those who do not follow Muhammad, and the duty to fight against all who do not believe and follow Muhammad.

Some of the negative aspects of Muhammad's example include:

- violence and warfare,
- murder,
- enslaving others,
- revenge and retribution,
- hatred,
- hatred of women,
- hatred of Jews,
- abuse,
- shame and shaming of others,

- intimidation,

- deception,

- taking offense,

- self-vindication,

- feelings of superiority,

- misrepresentation of God's character,

- the will to dominate others, and

- rape.

By reciting the *shahada* Muslims also endorse the Quran and *Sunna's* claims about Christ and the Bible. These include:

- denial of Christ's death on the cross;

- hatred of the cross;

- denial that Jesus is the Son of God (and curses upon those who believe this);

- the claim that Jews and Christians have corrupted their scriptures; and

- the claim that Jesus will return to destroy Christianity and force the whole world to submit to Muhammad's Sharia.

When someone leaves Islam, they should specifically reject and renounce the example of Muhammad, together with all the curses implied by the *shahada*. This means rejecting the belief that the Quran is the Word of God.

If the status of Muhammad as a Messenger is not explicitly renounced, then the curses and threats of the Quran, and Muhammad's opposition to the death of Christ and the Lordship of Christ can be a cause of spiritual instability, causing someone to be easily intimidated, and breed vulnerability and a lack of confidence as a follower of Jesus.

Prayer and Declaration for Renouncing the *shahada*

I renounce the false submission as taught and demonstrated by Muhammad.

I renounce and reject as false the belief that Muhammad is a messenger from God.

I reject the claim that the Quran is God's Word.

*I reject and renounce the **shahada** and every recitation of it.*

*I renounce saying **Al-Fatihah**. I renounce its claims that Jews are under the wrath of God, and Christians have gone astray.*

I renounce hatred of the Jews. I reject the claim that they have corrupted the Bible.

I reject the claim that God has rejected the Jews, and declare it to be a lie.

I renounce reciting the Quran and reject its authority over my life.

I renounce all false worship based on Muhammad's example.

I renounce all the false teachings about God which Muhammad brought, and the claim that Allah as portrayed in the Quran is God.

I renounce my dedication to Islam when I was born, and the dedication of my ancestors.

I specifically reject and renounce Muhammad's example. I renounce violence, intimidation, hatred, a spirit of offense,

111

deception, superiority, rape, abuse of women, theft and all the sins which Muhammad committed.

I reject and renounce shame. I declare that there is no condemnation in Christ Jesus and the blood of Christ cleanses me from all shame.

I reject and renounce all fear incited by Islam. I ask God's forgiveness for having entertained fears due to Islam, and choose to trust in the God and Father of my Lord Jesus Christ in all things.

I seek God's forgiveness for any and all the ungodly deeds I committed because of following Muhammad as a messenger of Allah.

*I reject and renounce the blasphemous claim that when Jesus returns he will compel all people on the earth to follow the **sharia** of Muhammad.*

I choose to follow Christ and him alone.

I confess that Christ is the Son of God, that he died on the cross for my sins, and was raised from the dead for my salvation. I praise God for the cross of Christ, and choose to take up my cross and follow him.

I confess that Christ is Lord of all. He rules over the heavens and the earth. He is Lord of my life. I confess that he will come again to judge the living and the dead. I cling to Christ and declare that there is no other name in heaven or on earth by which I must be saved.

I invite my Father God to give me a new heart, the heart of Christ, to guide me in all I do and say.

I reject all false worship, and dedicate my body to the worship of the living God, the Father, Son and Holy Spirit.

Freedom from Deception

Pastor Damanik, who was falsely imprisoned in Indonesia for speaking up against the Islamic *jihad*, said this about truth:

> ... although truth is difficult and very expensive we don't have any choice. We have to be willing to pay the expensive price. The alternative is to say goodbye to the truth. The truth lover has to fight extra hard to be someone with an iron will and at the same time be a person with a pure and transparent heart (like glass). The iron will is strong; it cannot be bent. It is unswerving in its commitment to truth ... The glass heart is one that is clean from one's own hidden interests and personal agenda. As with glass, the truth lover is sensitive and easily broken over the injustice and falsehood in the world. This broken-heartedness is not a sign of weakness, but it is a sign of strength and power. He is strong willed and his sharp mouth is able to speak out in the face of untruth and the falsehood of his surroundings. His heart cannot be still or quiet. His heart is always full of fight against injustice.

The fact that God is truthful is fundamental for us entering into relationship with him.

God is relational: he binds himself into relationships with humanity.

Abraham:

> 'I will establish my covenant as an everlasting covenant between me and you and your descendants after you for the generations to come, to be your God and the God of your descendants after you. The whole land of Canaan, where you are now an alien, I will give as an

everlasting possession to you and your descendants after you; and I will be their God.' (Genesis 17:7–8)

David:

You said, "I have made a covenant with my chosen one, I have sworn to David my servant, 'I will establish your line forever and make your throne firm through all generations.'" (Psalm 89:3–4)

God is unchanging and faithful to his relationships. He always keeps his word:

God is not a man, that he should lie, nor a son of man, that he should change his mind. Does he speak and then not act? Does he promise and not fulfill? (Numbers 23:19)

Give thanks to the Lord for he is good. His love endures forever. (Psalm 136)

[speaking of the Jews] ...as far as election is concerned, they are loved on account of the patriarchs, for God's gifts and his call are irrevocable. (Romans 11:28–29)

...a faith and knowledge resting on the hope of eternal life, which God, who does not lie, promised before the beginning of time... (Titus 1:2)

Because God wanted to make the unchanging nature of his purpose very clear to the heirs of what was promised, he confirmed it with an oath. God did this so that, by two unchangeable things in which it is impossible for God to lie, we who have fled to take hold of the hope offered to us may be greatly encouraged. We have this hope as an anchor for the soul, firm and secure. (Hebrews 6:17–19)

> But as surely as God is faithful, our message to you is not 'Yes' and 'No.' For the Son of God, Jesus Christ ... was not 'Yes' and 'No,' but in him it has always been 'Yes.' (2 Corinthians 1:18-20)

But in the Quran, this is not Allah's personality:

> Allah leads astray whomsoever He will, and he guides whomsoever he will; and he is the All-mighty, the All-wise. (Q14:4)

The true God of the Bible wants us to be like him:

> The Lord said to Moses, "Speak to the entire assembly of Israel and say to them: 'Be holy because I, the Lord your God, am holy.'" (Leviticus 19:1–2)

One of the ways we show God's holiness is by being truthful, living in truth, because God is true. Satan loves to put lies into our hearts. God's truth protects us:

> ... for your love is ever before me, and I walk continually in your truth. (Psalm 26:3)

> Into your hands I commit my spirit; redeem me, O Lord, the God of truth. (Psalm 31:5)

> Do not withhold your mercy from me, O Lord; may your love and your truth always protect me. (Psalm 40:11)

Truth cleanses us:

> Surely I was sinful at birth, sinful from the time my mother conceived me.
> Surely you desire truth in the inner parts; you teach me wisdom in the inmost place.
> Cleanse me with hyssop, and I will be clean; wash me, and I will be whiter than snow. (Psalm 51:5-7)

Jesus is full of truth:

> We have seen his glory, the glory of the One and Only, who came from the Father, full of grace and truth. (John 1:14)

We are called to walk, to live in truth:

> But whoever lives by the truth comes into the light, so that it may be seen plainly that what he has done has been done through God. (John 3:21)

In the gospels, Jesus says 'I tell you the truth' 78 times, and declares that we can only come to God through truth:

> God is spirit, and his worshipers must worship in spirit and in truth. (John 4:21)

> Jesus answered, 'I am the way and the truth and the life. No one comes to the Father except through me.' (John 14:6)

Paul speaks of the incompatibility between lying and following Christ:

> We also know that law is made not for the righteous but for lawbreakers and rebels, the ungodly and sinful, the unholy and irreligious; for those who kill their fathers or mothers, for murderers, for adulterers and perverts, for slave traders and liars and perjurers—and for whatever else is contrary to the sound doctrine that conforms to the glorious gospel of the blessed God, which he entrusted to me. (1 Timothy 1:9-11)

A cultural issue

According to Islam, lying is permitted under certain circumstances. God deceives people in the Quran.

Sometimes lying is obligatory. (See discussion of deception and *taqiyya* in *The Third Choice*, p.56ff).

Types of lies which Sharia law endorses include: lying in warfare, husbands lying to wives, lying to protect yourself, lying to defend the Umma, and self-protective lying (*taqiyya*) when Muslims believe they are in danger.

In Islam it is permitted to deny your faith (Q16:106), but a Christian cannot live this way:

> Whoever acknowledges me before men, I will also acknowledge him before my Father in heaven. But whoever disowns me before men, I will disown him before my Father in heaven. (Matthew 10:28-33)

Jesus said: 'Let your 'yes' be yes and your 'no' be no.

Prayer and Declaration for Deception

I thank you Father that you are a God of truth, that you shine your light into the darkest night. Today I choose not to live in darkness, but to dwell in your light.

Please forgive me for all the lies I have spoken. I have so often chosen the path of comfort and what is easy, not what is right. I ask you Lord to cleanse my lips from all ungodliness. Give me a heart which delights to hear the truth, and a mouth ready to make the truth known to others.

Give me courage to take comfort in the truth, and to reject the lies.

Today I reject and renounce the use of lies in my everyday life.

I reject all the teachings of Islam which are used to justify telling lies, including taqiyya. I choose to turn away from all lying and deception. I choose to live in the truth.

I declare that Jesus Christ is the Way, the Truth and the Life. I chose to live under the protection of his truth.

I declare that my security is in you, and the Truth shall set me free.

Please show me heavenly Father how to walk in the light of your truth. Give me the words to speak, and a way to walk in, which is based upon your Truth.

Freedom from Superiority and Entitlement

In Islam there is a great emphasis on superiority, on who is 'the best'. The Quran says that Muslims are better than non-Muslims:

> You are the best nation ever brought forth to men, bidding to honour, and forbidding dishonour, and believe in Allah. Had the People of the Book believed, it were better for them; some of them are believers, but the most of them are ungodly. (Q3:110)

And Islam is supposed to rule over other religions:

> It is He who has sent His Messenger with the guidance and the religion of truth, that He may cause it to triumph over every religion. (Q48:28)

There are also many hadiths of Muhammad which place a great emphasis on superiority.

The religion of Islam has had a deep influence on Arabic culture, shaping it over more than a thousand years. In Arabic cultures, concepts of 'honor' and 'shame' are very important, and people hate to be made to seem inferior. When there is conflict, there is often a recourse on humiliating others, and on seeking satisfaction for a sense of offense.

When someone leaves Islam, and decides to follow Christ, they need to renounce the emotional worldview in which a person needs to feel superior to those around them, and gains satisfaction from this.

The key to being released from this oppressive way of viewing the world is the example of Jesus Christ. This is beautifully expressed in the second chapter of Paul's Letter to the Philippians:

> If you have any encouragement from being united with Christ, if any comfort from his love, if any fellowship with the Spirit, if any tenderness and compassion, then make my joy complete by being like-minded, having the same love, being one in spirit and purpose. Do nothing out of selfish ambition or vain conceit, but in humility consider others better than yourselves. Each of you should look not only to your own interests, but also to the interests of others.
>
> Your attitude should be the same as that of Christ Jesus:
> Who, being in very nature God,
> did not consider equality with God something
> to be grasped,
> but made himself nothing,
> taking the very nature of a servant,
> being made in human likeness.
>
> And being found in appearance as a man,
> he humbled himself and became obedient to
> death— even death on a cross!
>
> Therefore God exalted him to the highest place
> and gave him the name that is above every name,

that at the name of Jesus every knee should bow,
in heaven and on earth and under the earth,
and every tongue confess that Jesus Christ is
Lord, to the glory of God the Father.
(Philippians 2)

From time to time a question came up among Jesus'
followers as to who was or would be the best among
them. They wanted to know who would have the place of
honor in Jesus' Kingdom.

> Then James and John, the sons of Zebedee, came to
> him. 'Teacher,' they said, 'we want you to do for us
> whatever we ask.'
>
> 'What do you want me to do for you?' he asked.
>
> They replied, 'Let one of us sit at your right and the
> other at your left in your glory.' ...
>
> When the ten heard about this, they became indignant
> with James and John. Jesus called them together and
> said, 'You know that those who are regarded as rulers
> of the Gentiles lord it over them, and their high
> officials exercise authority over them. Not so with
> you. Instead, **whoever wants to become great among
> you must be your servant, and whoever wants to be
> first must be slave of all**. For even the Son of Man
> did not come to be served, but to serve, and to give
> his life as a ransom for many.' (Mark 10:35-45)

When Jesus refers here to the 'gentiles', he means all the
nations. It is a universal trait of human nature to want to
feel important. Like James and John, human beings all
over the world seek the best seats or the places of greatest
honor. Jesus responds to this desire by explaining that if
his disciples truly want to follow him, they have to learn
how to serve others. In very practical ways, Jesus showed

how this worked. He 'made himself nothing' (Philippians 2:7), even to allowing himself to be crucified, the most disgraceful death known to people at his time.

The desire to be superior to others is a great trap for human beings. In the Garden of Eden, the snake tempted Eve with this, saying 'you will be like God' (Genesis 3:4). On this basis, Eve went along with what the snake wanted. A great deal of trouble and pain is caused in this world by people wanting to be superior to others.

The heart of Jesus is quite different. He chose to serve, not to dominate. He did not kill, but offered his life for others. The true follower of Christ does the same. He or she gains no pleasure from any sense of feeling superior. True Christ-followers are not afraid of shame or what other people think, because they trust in God to vindicate and protect them.

The danger of feeling superior comes out in the story of the prodigal son (Luke 15:11-32). The 'good' son felt himself to be superior and was unable to join his father's party for the long-lost son when he returned. For this he was rebuked by his father. The pathway to real success, in God's eyes, is to seek to serve others, not to lord it over them.

Prayer and Declaration for Superiority

I thank you Father that I am wonderfully made, because it is you who made me. Thank you that you love me and call me your own. Thank you for the privilege of following Jesus Christ.

Please forgive me for entertaining the desire to feel superior. I renounce and utterly reject such desires. I refuse to take comfort in feeling better than others. I acknowledge that I am a sinner, like everyone else, and I can accomplish nothing without you.

I also repent of and renounce feelings of belonging to a superior group or background. I confess that all peoples are equal in your sight.

I repent of uttering words of contempt for others and rejection of others, and seek your forgiveness for all these words.

I reject thinking less of people because of their race, their gender, their wealth, or their education.

I acknowledge that it is only by the grace of God that I can stand in your presence. I separate myself from all human judgement, and look to you alone to save me.

I specifically renounce Islam's teaching that the righteous are superior, that Islam makes people successful, and that Muslims are superior to non-Muslims.

I reject and renounce the claim that men are superior to women.

Heavenly Father, I turn away from every false sense of superiority and instead I choose to serve you.

Lord I also choose to rejoice in the successes of others. I reject and renounce all envy and jealousy of others.

Lord please give me a sound and accurate judgement about who I am in you. Teach me the truth of how you see me. Help me to be content as the person you have created me to be.

Bibliography

Bernard, J.H. 1928. *A critical and exegetical commentary on the Gospel according to John.* 2 vols. Edinburgh: T&T Clark.

Carson, D.A. 1991. *The Gospel according to John.* Leicester, England: Inter-Varsity Press.

Gibson, Noel and Phyl. 1987. *Evicting demonic squatters and breaking bondages.* Drummoyne, NSW: Freedom in Christ Ministries Trust. (An earlier edition of *Evicting demonic intruders.*)

Houlden, J.H. 1970. *Paul's letters from prison: Philippians, Colossians, Philemon and Ephesians.* Harmondsworth, Middlesex: Penguin.

Kreider, Alan. 1995. *Worship and Evangelism in Pre-Christendom.* Alcuin/GROW Joint Liturgical Studies, 32. Cambridge: Grove Books Ltd.

Muir, William. 1861. *The life of Mahomet.* London: Smith, Elder and Co.

Made in the USA
Columbia, SC
24 December 2017